HOW TO
TALK
TO ANYONE

Communicate with Confidence and Charisma,

Using Charm, Banter and Better Small Talk

LUCAS BAILEY

Your FREE Bonuses

Download the following eBooks for free to supplement your learning.

Bonus 1:

5 Strategies for Effective Online Networking

Discover How to:

- Decide where to network
- Connect with the right people
- Build and nurture your online network
- … and more

Bonus 2:

The 8 Secrets of Great Public Speaking

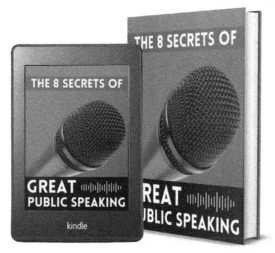

Discover How to:

- Prepare yourself before hand
- Calm any nervousness you may feel
- Confidently deliver a great speech
- ... and more

Scan the QR Code with your cell phone to gain access:

"Communication is the number one skill we all need to improve, whether in the workplace or at home. It doesn't matter if you have an audience of 1 or 1 million, connection should be the goal of any kind of communication. Communicating for the sake of communicating won't help build or strengthen relationships, connecting will."

- DAVID TYLER

Download the Audio Version of this Book for FREE

If you love listening to audiobooks on-the-go or would enjoy a narration as you read along, I have a great news for you. You can download the full audiobook version of *How to Talk to Anyone* for FREE (Regularly $14.95) just by signing up for a FREE 30-day Audible trial with one of the links below!

Scan a QR Code Below to Get Started:

Audiobook US   Audiobook UK

Contents

HOW TO

TALK

TO ANYONE

INTRODUCTION

Interacting with each other is fundamental to the human experience, but it eludes many of us. Some feel unprepared to communicate in the adult world, due to cultural differences, the inability to read social cues, or plain old shyness. We have enabled screens to act as a poor substitute for real human interaction, resulting in arrested development in our emotional and social intelligence.

The first thing we have to realize is that becoming a social butterfly is something that can be practiced. "Repetition is the mother of skill" should be everyone's mantra.

You picked up this book because you need help navigating the maze of human interaction. You will learn how to read cues from others and actively listen. Only then can you master presenting yourself, talking and behaving at work, out on the town, with family, and in small groups. For some, skills like selling, banter, inspiring, writing, flirting, and diffusing tension seem to come easily. Once you know *how* they accomplish this, you might surprise yourself with how far you will go.

Now you may be saying to yourself:

You can't just willpower your way into success.

Collecting Role Models: Arnold Schwarzenegger

No other person exemplifies the power of confidence more than Arnold Schwarzenegger. This is a man who, as comedian Bill Burr put it, "should be unloading trucks in Transylvania". Instead, he believed in himself enough to move to America with twenty dollars to his name and made a career out of bodybuilding.

There he learned how to work the crowd, manufacture tension, and get people invested in a previously unnamed sport. He reached the top of the mountain by becoming Mr. Olympia but he was not satisfied. He decided to pursue acting despite his heavy accent and zero Hollywood connections.

The odds were stacked against him; having an accent often hinders making it in the media, and most successful actors are born into Hollywood families. While he did work with acting and speech coaches, he did not wait until he trained enough to sound like James Bond. He succeeded and became one of the highest-grossing action stars through charisma, and he recognized his unique traits as an opportunity to brand himself.

He then became governor of California and, compared to later celebrity political attempts, did a decent job. While he has had his ups and downs, Arnold remains a role model for everyone with the chips stacked against them. He is personable, humble, and radiates a positivity that leaves you hooked on every word he says. If you want to study that level of confidence, he should be one of the first people you go to.

Why You Might Have Trouble Talking

We like to break people into two groups: introverts and extroverts. Introverts tend to be exhausted by prolonged socialization. This does not mean they hate everyone. Quite the contrary, introverts maintain rewarding social lives and enjoy events; they just need a recharge afterward. Think of it like flexing a muscle, yeah, it looks good, but you can't maintain it and need to relax. Extroverts can withstand the exhaustion that comes with socializing. They seem to have been born with the "charming gene", but they just sought more social opportunities and are well-practiced.

Then we have the two extremes, the charismatic types that are a combination of confident and highly socially intelligent to the point that you would follow them, and those with extreme social anxiety. This goes beyond shyness or a fear of public speaking. This is an intense aversion to social interaction based on the unfounded fear of judgment. Social anxiety can rob you of opportunities and cost you friendships and even your job if it manifests severely. It is your prefrontal cortex going into crisis mode every time you interact with people, paralyzing you both physically and mentally. While this book will help with communication, getting to the root of your anxiety with a therapist or a trusted colleague is highly encouraged.

While this book may trigger some unpleasant memories of a past failure to be charming or breaking out in hives when you were asked to talk in a meeting, it is essential to note that these are not character failings or weaknesses. If you have the notion that you are unworthy of love or friendship–the only way you will improve is to let that go. There is a difference between self-reflection and punishing yourself. It's time to recognize that voice in your head telling you that you deserve to be alone, and that self-improvement is a fantasy is not helpful and is not your friend. Psychologically, they will eventually pivot from self-criticism to self-hatred (Werner et al., 2019). You will never be able to effectively help yourself if you hate yourself. The first lesson here; be kind to yourself.

In my two decades of coaching, I have helped many men and women get out of their way and see their true potential. Whether it's people who have trouble professionally, romantically, socially, or all three, there is a way out. You must believe you can improve when you are charming people with all the new skills you have learned. You don't need to become a loudmouth or a

INTRODUCTION

Stepford smiler; you need to be able to share the best version of yourself. The stories I am about to share are based on my clients' experiences. Names and other identifying details have been altered for privacy.

HOW TO READ PEOPLE

AND MAKE SURE THEY READ THE BEST VERSION OF YOU

"Training yourself to communicate effectively opens many doors both personally and professionally. People tend to trust you more, as well as take you seriously."

- TEO VANYO

First Impressions Are Everything

Monica's lab mates have invited her to one of their biweekly happy hours to blow off some steam. This was a surprise because if she had to guess, her coworkers were professional, reserved, and only wanted to talk about work. However, after the first round, Monica realized the point of these happy hours. She immediately noticed some changes in their presence while they spoke to her.

The youngest, Caroline, who usually looked uptight, with her shoulders tense, wide eyes, and tight mouth, was suddenly smiling, standing tall, and using her hands more when she talked.

Her coworker Bill, who was in his mid-thirties and had the demeanor of a drill sergeant, took off his tie, undid the first button on his collar, made dad jokes, and passionately talked about his research. Mary, the oldest, who Monica assumed despised her thanks to her pursed lips, hands-on-hip posture, and intense eye contact, was suddenly very maternal and doling out advice on how to thrive in the new company.

Monica had entirely misjudged all of them based on their body language, but who could blame her? Seeing them in a new light gave her hope of fitting into and leading the team.

Body language and appearance are our first introduction to people. Before we get a chance to say "hello", we have told a thousand stories about how we present ourselves. Picture this, you walk into a bar and see two people, one dressed nicely and smiling as he chats with the bartender. You assume he is well adjusted, successful and friendly. You see someone else with a wrinkled shirt, red-faced, and scowling.

One would be forgiven for thinking you are there to drown away your sorrows. Which one would you approach first to talk about the game? While it takes effort, knowing how to enter a room is the first step to letting people in and hopefully being charmed.

Becoming Aware of Your Body

"You got your looks, your pretty face, and don't underestimate the importance of body language, HA!"
– Ursula, *Little Mermaid*

Did you just sit up straight when the subject of bodily awareness came up? Don't worry, it's normal. You must practice good body language to the point where it becomes second nature. This does not mean invoking your inner boot camp cadet and standing up so straight that your bones crack. People like to be relaxed and take to people who facilitate that. There is a balance between appealing body language and overcompensating. Good body language has some pretty universal rules:

- Stand up straight with your shoulders rolled slightly back

- Keep your head up (physically and mentally)

- Keep your hands visible, not behind you or in your pockets. Humans are evolutionarily predisposed to see this as a showing of peace.

- Keep your legs shoulder-width apart.

- Stand squared off with the person.

- Never hold a bag or a drink directly in front of you; this can be seen as guarding and is a sign that you do not want people in your space.

Learn how to mirror. Mirroring is adopting the speech and mannerisms of the person we interact with. We understand, copy, bond, and look for validation through mirroring. It works because we like it when things are familiar. We know ourselves; we can predict how we will respond and project those biases onto someone that resembles us. It's the fast track to establishing rapport that is purely subconscious.

- Stand square with the person (like a mirror)
- If they use an uncommon word like *gosh* or stress certain syllables, mimic that.
- Match the level of gesturing a person does with their hands.
- Match their energy or, with more practice, guide their energy. If a person is more subdued, it would be beneficial to talk quieter and use more subtle movements; likewise, if a person is laughing, at least smile along.

While you need to mirror the other person so they ingratiate themselves to you, it is a two-way street; they will mirror you. If you are a pleasant person to be around, that becomes infectious, and they will leave the interaction with a good feeling. However, if you are nervous, angry, or are a downer, even if the person started off in a good mood, they may be left exhausted by the interaction because they have taken in that negativity.

Don't Blink

Eye contact can also be a delicate task. The border between a confident stare that spells intrigue and personality and a creepy stare is razor-thin. Bad eye contact can look like this:

- Opening your eyes too wide

- Not blinking

- Staring for too long (if a person has noticed you, do not keep the stare going for more than a second, they will see)

- Looking angry while staring

- Smiling while staring

Prolonged eye contact, for some, can also be exhausting. There is a particular vulnerability that comes with eye contact, and it is akin to an invasion of personal space. It is worth noting that for some neurodivergent people, such as those with autism, eye contact can be extremely difficult or sometimes impossible to maintain, but adjustments can be made to support and improve upon this, whether it's you yourself, or the person that you're communicating with who is finding eye contact difficult. Just like training for a marathon, the key is to practice consistently and learn to build up over a period of time.

Breaking eye contact once it is established can be seen a sign of weakness, not only for us but also in the animal kingdom. If you have ever watched a testosterone-fueled stare-down at a UFC fight, you will understand a human's relationship between eye contact and dominance.

Reading Other People Like a Book

You are only one part of the equation. To gauge your level of interaction, you need to read people. This is not a true crime show where the psychologist character can tell if a person wet the bed as a child because of the way they sit. However, some pretty big visual cues can give you a peek into what is happening in someone's head and how your conversation skills are progressing. Signs that a person might be uncomfortable include:

- Standing at an angle; in an effort to look smaller.
- They may start to step away.
- Hands in pockets
- Head down
- Walking leading with your head instead of your chest

If you get to a conversation, figuring out when to break off is essential. People are not good at knowing when to stop talking. They are either too ingrained in their stories to stop, fear offending someone by cutting the interaction short, or fear overstaying their welcome and breaking off too early. You can read when a person is starting to disengage if you know what to look for:

- If you realize you have been talking for a long time without the other person interjecting

- Answers become one word or variations of "mhhm, okay", and the occasional head nod

- The other person starts to step away

- Mentions of different plans or time constraints start

- Their eyes start to unfocus

It happens to all of us, and that is okay. However, if you are too self-absorbed in your own story to notice these signs, it can make a wrong impression on a person. The reality is that people need help seeing when it is time to end a conversation. It is better to leave a person wanting more than overstaying your welcome. You can always circle back to the person and if you are feeling bold, ask for some contact information.

Physical Contact

Knowing when to give and how to receive physical contact is the bane of some people's existence. Do you know what it feels like when someone gives you an unwanted shoulder slap or touches you for a bit too long? No one wants to be known as the handsy person.

There are different thresholds for distance and contact depending on culture and situation. American and most European cultures value personal space. Touching is often seen as something reserved for very close friends and family. Meanwhile, Latin American and some Middle Eastern cultures have a much smaller personal bubble. A hug and even a kiss are standard greetings even amongst strangers. There are situations, though, where physical contact is beneficial. We will start with the universal form of human communication, the handshake.

Handshakes

Handshakes are a fascinating quirk of western society. It first came about in ancient Greece and was widely adopted because, unlike bowing or curtseying, it puts you on the same playing field as the other person. Some theorize that it is a way for humans to collect smell signals from other people. Regardless of the reason, mastering the handshake will help with that all-important first impression. This simple greeting says a lot about someone's personality.

People tend to maintain their handshake throughout their lives if their overall predisposition stays constant. An introvert may have a limp handshake that can be subject to ridicule, while an extrovert will have a firmer handshake. For women, there is another dimension, despite the idea that women's handshakes will be more docile. A more educated woman tends to have a firmer grip than one that is either uneducated or traditional.

Handshakes get people to like us. Studies show that greeting with a handshake reduces avoidance behaviors during an interaction, indicating a level of comfort. Brain scans also revealed that a handshake sends a signal to the nucleus accumbens, or in layman's terms, the brain's reward center.

So what makes a good handshake? It's about grip, technique, and duration. On the scale of dead fish to Donald Trump attempting to rip the arm off of a world leader, you want to fall around the middle or slightly above.

- Maintain a good grip, just enough to show that you feel good about the interaction without trying to break their fingers. Match their grip so you can maintain your fingers wrapped around their hand.

- Do not approach the handshake with your palm down; keep it facing medially

- Cup your palm, don't lay it flat against the other person's palm

- Shake from your elbow; not the wrist. Your arm is a much more effective anchor point if you want to avoid noodle arm.

- Do not pull in so much. You risk throwing a person off balance.

- Maintain eye contact during the handshake

- Step away from the person once the handshake is complete

Handshakes tend to hit diminishing returns after the three-second mark. Shorter handshakes are okay, but you don't maximize those psychological benefits if you keep it brief. A crushing handshake can come off as either awkward or downright insufferable. It's a petty power move designed to intimidate, defeating the handshake's original intent. For the rest of the interaction, the person will have an aching hand to remind them of an inappropriate attempt to dominate. Remember, powerful people don't need to show their strength; they prove it with tangible results. Only an insecure person who brings nothing to the table would attempt this impotent display.

Closing the Gap While Respecting Someone Else's Space

If you are trying to get close to a stranger, there are ways to create an illusion of intimacy (note, this does not mean sexual, this means a deeper level of connection). This is how politicians and overall charismatics win people over easily and quickly. This is all second nature for some, but it can be learned.

In its final form, this is known as *The Reality Distortion Effect* or the tornado of charisma that can sweep people off their feet and make them putty in someone else's hands. People capable of this have gone on to become president, start cults, and make effective con artists. One of the most famous examples of this is Bill Clinton. While this quality eventually returned to haunt him, it initially made his political career. People described talking to Clinton at a campaign event or a dinner, and even though they were in a crowded room, Clinton made them feel like they were the only two people on the face of the planet. He has been lauded for his extraordinary memory, meeting someone on the campaign trail, coming back a year later, and remembering details about that person's life. People that hated everything he stood for walked away begrudgingly liking him.

Charisma may have nothing to do with the issues, but it inspires trust and authority. While getting to the level of Bill Clinton or Steve Jobs may take a lot of practice, you can do some simple things to bridge the chasm from strangers to blossoming friendships.

You have to find a balance or risk overwhelming the other person. There is a push and pull between distance, volume, and contact. You can use one to compensate for distance or lack of another or enhance the conversation. Making the mistake of turning up the dial on all these at once will make you appear obnoxious.

- Once again, square up, so you take up as much of their field of vision as possible. You are all that exists.

- If you want to close the distance physically without making the other person uncomfortable, approach from the side. Our level of personal space can be measured in feet from the front but inches from the side. It's why you can tolerate a long car ride with your family without becoming claustrophobic.

- If you have to maintain distance, speak louder and clearer.

- If you are in a crowded place and are physically very close to each other, speak softly and be wary of your topic of conversation; keep it positive and light.

- Whispering close to someone's ear in a loud room is a romantic way to overcome volume.

- Get the person to discuss their opinions and lives and engage with those topics. Treat them as a human with experiences and perspectives you would like to know more about, not an object.

You can see where the tightrope act becomes apparent. If you are in close proximity, like at an intimate bar, speaking loudly can look intimidating, but it is more acceptable if you are across a wide table. If you are getting deep into the weeds of a personal conversation, speaking too loud shows a lack of tact. Intense eye contact can get someone reaching for the pepper spray if you are in an enclosed space like an elevator.

Remember that you are using intimacy to bridge one form of distance present when you are strangers. You might not be at the point where you feel comfortable standing too close or touching them, but you can make them feel your presence despite that. They get used to you and will let down their guard a bit so long as you don't mess it up.

Key Takeaways

- Before you know it, people will judge you based on your appearance and body language. Make this first impression count!

- Reading others, not speaking, is the first step in learning how to communicate. People leave things unsaid, but you can work to fill in those blanks.

- You can determine whether a person wants to keep conversing or end the conversation through body language. Oblige them and leave them wanting more.

- Physical contact is a delicate game, but it can increase effective communication. Handshakes are a universal greeting; you need to hold your ground without unintentionally coming off as a bully.

- Closing a distance gap, whether a physical distance, volume, or emotional, can be achieved subtly.

Now that we have set ourselves up for success by recognizing not only our own presence but the presence of others, it is time to work on the most challenging part of a conversation, getting it going.

GET THEM TALKING

"Once you communicate, you don't discover reality, you create reality."

- MEIR EZRA

After moving from Norway, Arthur was itching to socialize in a new city. He decided to go to a cozy bar next to the office to try and make some friends or even find a girl to woo. Arthur is a decent-looking guy, not Chris Evans hot, but he's dated multiple times before, and his mom lets him know how handsome he is every time she sees him. That has to count for something.

There's just one problem. Arthur has always had his best friend to be his wingman back home. He needed that extra hype to help clear his path of anything that may obstruct him on his way to talking to a girl he finds cute. Now he's all alone, and he is at a loss in a new city that, unlike him, valued small talk and physical contact.

Arthur settled in at the bar. A young woman seats herself across from him. He makes his move.

Arthur: Hey, you have pretty eyes.

Woman #1: I'm waiting for my boyfriend.

Arthur was rattled; he didn't think he was out of practice but was shut down immediately. Arthur orders a drink and waits for the next girl to try and chat up.

Arthur: This is a nice place, don't you think?

Woman #2: ...yes.

The pause was deafening, and his mind blanked. He had no idea what to say, and by the time he thought of something, the girl was rejoined by her friend, and the window had closed. He tried again but was visibly getting frustrated.

Arthur: You must find this place boring too.

Woman #3: I actually really like this place.

Arthur finished his drink and got out of there; his first foray into the city was a dud. Arthur knew he was good at talking once he was comfortable, but that first hurdle always gave him trouble. He needed to change his approach if he didn't want his old wingman to be attached to his hip until he married a girl.

Opening the Conversational Can of Worms

The most intimidating point of a conversation is the start. We never know what direction it will go, and the stakes feel higher with strangers. A negative interaction can have you clam up for years. So how do you start and continue a conversation? In this world of fast clicks and short-form content, people's tolerance for discussion takes a nosedive if it is not engaging. Your mileage may vary as each person on the other side can have a different level of social anxiety, stress, or any other factor that might stifle their ability to engage.

Getting Your Foot Through the Door

The start of the conversation is make or break time. You have to make your opener count, or the chances of the conversation going further will go away. The first rule is to avoid cliches such as:

That's some weather outside, huh?

What do you do?

Do you live around here?

These questions are boring and done to death. The weather is not exactly a riveting subject when first meeting someone (unless you are both taking shelter in a rainstorm). Avoid occupations for a little while. Odds are, if a person is single, it is the first question they are asked every time. Location-based questions are also a miss. It is invasive when meeting a stranger; it might kick a person into defensive mode. Also, it is a simple yes or no question. Small talk, in general, is under-stimulating and stifling.

One of the cardinal rules of good conversation is that it needs to move back and forth like a game of ping-pong. A question with a dichotomous answer is not particularly engaging. Instead, go for a tantalizing statement or an open-ended question that will be a road map to stimulating conversation. Remember to ramp up to the deep end of the conversation pool. Do not go in too hard with intense questions, emotions, or statements at first, even if you think it's complimentary. The conversation should be like a slow dance at first, each swaying back and forth with the music, taking turns leading, not stepping on a landmine. To avoid the landmine on the first step, you should avoid bringing up:

- Politics

- Personal finances

- Religion

- Family issues

- Intense stories from your past

- Invasive questions

- Being overtly sexual or implying anything other than general attraction

You can venture into these topics later but for now, keep it light. It might be tempting to vent to an unsuspecting person, but the results can be awkward. It can make a person feel uncomfortable and like you have huge expectations of them within the first five minutes of the meeting. You should avoid strong statements in the positive direction as well.

I think I love you.

You have a gorgeous body.

I just look at you, and I see the answer to all of my problems.

You should also avoid being presumptuous about a person, especially if it is a negative assumption. Phrases like:

Everyone else here is a loser, don't you think?

Oof, you have to do that sort of work...you must hate your job!

It is tempting to make a person feel special, but you have nothing to base this opinion on, and it says more about you than the other person. Never let your first impression be petty, negative, or arrogant; even if that is not your intention, you will have to do a lot of work to undo that.

You have to be engaging and leave the door open to wanting more. Do not start simple, but do start easy. You can give a compliment, but a good rule of thumb is not to praise something they were born with. Instead, compliment something they chose, like her hairstyle, clothes, or drink. Men report they don't hear compliments nearly enough. Men can ride the high for a year if you admire how he styles his beard. Giving a man respectful praise might fast-track you on the relationship train.

They respond to the compliment and even return one; now what? The door is cracked open, but there are plenty of ways to still slam it shut. Keep the conversation steady but slowly intensifying. You can pepper probing questions as you go, and you will have more to work with as you get more information.

Jeremy arrived late to the happy hour that Monica was attending. She did not know what to make of the shy man. He was quiet, kept his hands in his pockets, and often mumbled when he talked. Monica had been surprised by her other coworkers; she might as well extend the same courtesy to Jeremy. Monica knew that talking about work would fail since that's all they had talked about thus far. She decided to try a different strategy, noticing his shirt with the Star Wars rebellion symbol on it.

Monica: I like your shirt.

Jeremy: Oh, thanks. Do you like Star Wars?

Monica: I've seen Empire Strikes Back easily a hundred times, it's my favorite movie. Which is yours!

Jeremy: Revenge of the Sith is my favorite but Empire is a close second.

Monica: Yeah I had a crush on Anakin in those movies...of course, before he became a Sith!

Jeremy had laughed; Monica had never seen that before.

Monica: What did you think of Rise of Skywalker?

Jeremy: I only saw it out of obligation; it was awful!

Monica: Right?!

Monica connected with Jeremy on a deeper level just by using the information on his shirt. You should also use your surroundings. If a person is singing along with, or just enjoying the jukebox rendition of *It's Not Unusual,* join in on the fun, especially if you are at a bar which is one of the most acceptable places to talk to a stranger.

Embrace your inner networking event coordinator and have some creative icebreaker questions in the barrel. You can always preface them by saying:

I have a weird question I ask everyone I first meet.

Remember, these need to be fun but challenging. Avoid easy cliches like:

Would you rather fight a hundred duck-sized horses or one horse-sized duck?

What is a fun fact about yourself?

Instead, go for:

What is your favorite quality about yourself?

What was the most challenging part about moving here?

Could you fight your father in his prime?

These questions invite one of the prominent trust-builders; vulnerability. If you prove to them that you are worth getting to know, people will open up to you. Avoid intense stories or bringing up your ex to make yourself vulnerable. A mildly embarrassing story about how you humiliated yourself at the annual hot sauce festival or when you called the teacher "mommy" tells a person that you are willing to open up as well. You might be regaled by an equally amusing story about the other person getting a baby tooth knocked out by a kickball.

That conversation snowball is growing, and soon you might start to form the seeds of a bond. Those probing questions and icebreakers are great for getting to the emotional root of a person's life. It is not enough to say you sympathize with a person; you must empathize.

New jobs are tough sometimes. I know you can handle it, but that doesn't change the fact that it's an intimidating environment.

Awwww, your dog looks so cute in his Halloween costume! It looks like you take great care of him and give him lots of love.

This is not making a baseless assumption; this is taking their conversations and the emotions behind them and validating them. You also don't have to agree with a person's actions or opinions. It's about *understanding* why a person might have that perspective that makes you a great communicator. Putting into words an emotion that a person might not think they are expressing (but are betraying with tone and body language) makes someone feel seen and understood. That is how you get into someone's good graces and potentially into their heart.

Key Takeaways

- Starting the conversation is hard but don't settle for simple small talk. It is unfulfilling and rarely leads to anything else.

- Be creative and ask open-ended questions so the conversation flows.

- Use their interests to get the conversation going then you can pivot into a topic you both enjoy once you have enough information.

- Conversations should be fun, so do not go in too strong. Build momentum slowly so your guest is not overwhelmed.

AT HOME, AT WORK, AT PLAY

"The art of communication is the language of leadership."

- JAMES HUMES

Talking on the Job

When dealing with your superiors, you need to ask yourself, *what is my future in this job*? If you plan to get in and out in a few years, your approach will be more straightforward. The goal is to get a good reference letter and make your work experience somewhat positive. You need to prove that you are a respectful and competent worker.

It is a different story if you are moving up the ladder. You will have to play into company politics, get to know people, and have confidence in doing so. Once you make it to the top, the real battle begins; becoming an effective leader.

Universal Rules for Socializing at Work

This one goes without saying but be respectful of everyone, not just those you stand to gain from. This does not mean getting walked all over, but engaging in a few pleasantries will get you on everyone's nice list. Simply acknowledging someone when they enter a room is enormous. The conversation does not have to continue beyond that, but that simple act can make someone feel seen and like they are wanted in that space. You might even make a few allies that way.

No one likes a suck-up. The quickest way to get on your coworkers' shit list is to be sickeningly sweet and complimentary to only those above you. You want to be a force for positivity in the workplace for everyone. You will quickly become a chore to work with, and everyone will dread seeing your name on the schedule. Work can be challenging, but you need to avoid phrases like:

Eh, the janitor will get it later!

Ugh, why am I doing this? Isn't that why we have interns?

I don't take notes, get a secretary or one of the girls to do it.

This place sucks!

I want to go home!

Offices are rife with drama, and people always want to get in on the piping hot tea. Nothing will perk up Cathy in accounting faster than the latest rumor about Joel in IT dating an intern or how someone discovered Sandra's social media (put a pin in this one). If you are saying something at work, it is safer to assume everyone will hear it and have an opinion. This also applies to positive attributes such as a skill unrelated to your job description. Management can increase your responsibilities without increasing your pay. Why would they hire someone else to design their website when you can do it while handling all your other duties? Keep it under your hat for an emergency when you can save the day.

You should aim to have some friends at work, since you are spending forty hours a week with these people! However, there is a lot at stake if things go wrong. With a regular friend, if you fall out, then you never have to see them again. With work friends, you are tied to that person until one of you quits or transfers. Workplace relationships should start slowly. You can commiserate over your jobs, go out to happy hours, and lean on each other for support when things go wrong. However, a high degree of trust needs to be earned. You don't want something you may have told someone in confidence to be used against you.

- Don't talk about future plans if they do not involve the company.

- Don't speak negatively about a coworker or another department or engage in gossip; your opinion on the matter might spread around to the wrong person.

- DO NOT TALK ABOUT YOUR SEX LIFE. If you wouldn't say it to your mother, don't say it to your coworkers. After a few work-sponsored happy hour drinks, it can be tempting to make the conversation fun, but some things, especially those that can end up as a sexual harassment claim, should be avoided at all costs.

- If you have a crush on someone or find them attractive, keep it to yourself.

In these cases, keeping people at arm's length can go a long way in keeping you out of trouble. You may see these people for forty hours a week, but venting to them like a therapist will yield disastrous results more often than not.

Meeting Dynamics

Meetings are often the worst part of every job. That is not by design; most people don't know how to conduct them. Meetings should be where issues are discussed with relevant people, synergy leads to creative ideas, and workplace camaraderie can grow. It has become a waste of time and money in the modern corporate world. But employees feel like they have to show their face and attend. In the end, you have people frustrated about their deadlines, not contributing, and having their workflow interrupted. Still, as much as we hate to admit it, good meetings are essential to any business and product development. Information sharing through effective meetings is required for communicating consistent messages.

Meetings don't just last their allotted hour, there is meeting prep, cutting tasks short so they do not overlap, grabbing coffee, walking over (unless it's on zoom), and the dead time before the meeting starts. Then after a bad meeting, you have the traditional post-meeting venting session where coworkers talk about how they should not have had to go to that meeting. So how do you make meetings more productive, how do you keep things on track, and how do you deal with interruptions?

Meeting dynamics have the usual cast of characters and dysfunctions.

- There is inter-department squabbling; Engineering wants it done right, but sales wants it done fast, and finance wants it done cheap. Everyone had a different vision for the same goal, and they understandably want to protect their team.

- The gunners pick apart every problem, flaw, or disagreement in the most public way possible to prove how smart they are.

- Some shy ones seem to have a lot to say but can't bring themselves to vocalize their concerns.

- The managers monopolize the conversation and redirect back onto themselves, regardless of the agenda.

- Finally, the well-meaning excitable one constantly interrupts to share an idea.

The first thing to determine is if there should even be a meeting. As a manager, is this a call you can make yourself? Can it be solved with a casual five-minute chat or in an email? While meetings may seem informal to management (because they go to so many of them), meetings can be an event to lower staff. Centering a topic around an issue can inflate its level of importance. Save the conference room reservations for the consequential stuff where you need a natural flow of ideas. This is where creativity and imagination occur. Situations that do call for a meeting include:

- Project design meetings with management. This is where the overall design of the project, discussion on deadlines, delegation, finances, foreseeable chokepoints and pitfalls, resource allocation, and contingency plans are worked out.

- Kick-off meetings where everyone touching a project gathers. Scope, expectations, pipelines, and responsibilities are discussed. There is a better time for Jenny on the lab team to bring up that she needs a replacement pipette.

- Casual team meetings can be used for more minor issues, low-level planning, or if there is something management missed during the project development phase.

- Emergency meetings where significant issues that impact the entire team or have downstream consequences are handled.

- Meetings to celebrate when a big project wraps up successfully can include a debrief section where strengths and weaknesses are discussed.

Think about it this way; if you can foresee the email chain of a certain topic stretching for several days, it needs to be a meeting.

So how do you have a productive meeting where everyone feels heard? Consider the purpose of the meeting: information sharing, planning, guest speaker, annual financial statement. Once you know the purpose, create an agenda. That way, you can determine the attendees more easily. Only include those with a vested interest in attending. Make sure you allow sufficient time for introductions at the beginning, and a wrap-up or next steps at the end.

A three hour meeting about the financial forecast may not be the best use of employees' time. Consider sending pre-meeting data via email, then limiting the in-person meeting to a brief presentation of the material, along with a question and answer session. Sending meeting minutes, or summaries, is useful for the stakeholders unable to attend.

Monica: *Thanks for coming today! Let's discuss the issues in the project pipeline. Since Mike is the lab manager, I want him to review the process thoroughly; then, as the head of QC, Meghan can discuss why and how the results have failed. Since the analysts are physically handling everything, I also need your perspective. Let's solve this problem.*

You have to establish the conduct you expect at your meetings. Shut down interruptions immediately, even if they are valid; there is a time and place, and you need to normalize this expectation.

Caroline: *So the temperature is set at 45 degrees celsius and-*

Daniel: *Wait, the protocol says that the incubator should be set at 40 degrees Celsius-*

Monica: *Hang on, Daniel, let her finish her thought (gently). You were saying, Caroline?*

Caroline: *We chose that temperature when we optimized the protocol.*

Daniel: *Oh*

For most people, getting called out on interrupting is enough to get them to stop. Other phrases you can use include:

That's a good point, but let me finish here, and we can circle back to that.

That's important, but that goes beyond the scope of this meeting, and we don't have much time; we can discuss it after we let everyone else go.

Notice that none of these diminish the point someone clse is making, but at the same time, it emphasizes that someone else has the floor and needs to be respected. It is diplomatic, validates the interrupter and the speaker so they are not insulted, and keeps the meeting on track.

Simply extending your hand out gently can add to this. It translates as a nice "stop what you are doing" that works on most people, including children. This, combined with a calm, quiet voice, is effective. You should avoid making this motion quickly as it can translate into "shut up" instead. Other gestures you should avoid are placing your pointer finger on your mouth and shushing a person, closing your hand like a mouth, or waving your pointer finger. Even if the other person deserves it, the air of condescension will only increase tension.

If interruptions continue to be a common problem, you will have to be the jerk for the team's sake. Employ a physical symbol that allows a person to speak like the conch in *Lord of the Flies*. It's childish, but it can also encourage others to talk since there is no fear of interruption. You can also just limit questions and comments until everyone has spoken. It creates a clear boundary for all to respect.

Communicating At Home

Family is the most important circle with which we surround ourselves. We take them for granted since we are stuck with each other until we hit a breaking point. Many parents see children as an extension of themselves and cannot deal with that child not meeting expectations. Many couples start making assumptions about each other and are blinded to cracks in their relationship. They selectively block out criticism and cries for help until one can't take it anymore and files for divorce.

Collecting Role Models: Gomez and Morticia Addams

Gomez and Morticia Addams have the perfect marriage. They were revolutionary when they debuted on TV in 1964. The show is about a weird, creepy family that kept spiders, and carnivorous plants, participated in fencing and made friends with monsters. They were at odds with their Anglo-Saxon neighbors, who saw them as a collection of freaks rather than a well-adjusted family.

Gomez and Morticia encouraged their children's interests and stepped in when they went too far. Other television couples played dysfunction up for laughs. *The Honeymooners'* Ralph regularly threatened Alice with physical violence. On several occasions, the titular character in *I Love Lucy* was bent over her husband's knee and spanked.

Gomez and Morticia were a complete departure from that. They remained attracted to each other after years of marriage and constantly vocalized it. They respected each other as equals seeking counsel with the person they trusted most. Despite their passion for each other, they were not attached at the hip; Gomez had his trains, and Morticia had her flower arranging.

They were compatible in the places that matter most. As a result, their love remained and grew as their family did. They were each other's biggest cheerleaders and support system as they ran into issues fitting in with society. Despite their morbid tastes, they were both infectiously positive and saw the good in everyone. This relationship would not be possible if it were around the usual framework of a nagging wife and belligerent husband that is shoved down our throats. If you need a romance to aspire to, forget Edward and Bella, The Notebook, and most modern sitcoms; instead look to the kooky Addams Family.

Talking with Kids

Monica loved her family, but in hindsight, many mistakes were made when she and her siblings were raised. Her parents were stressed and impoverished, had short fuses, and were often too blunt. They did not have the mental capacity to consider that their kids weren't tiny adults; they were young children that were sensitive, impulsive, and, gasp, immature. A distinct lack of empathy manifested differently as each of the siblings grew up. Monica, for example, became a people pleaser. The parents put food on the table and did their best to quell their frustration, but it was the children who suffered when they failed:

- Ignoring how issues affect children emotionally.
- Putting on a strong front and never showing vulnerability.
- Viewing anger as a direct challenge rather than an outlet for a more significant issue.
- Never explaining their reasoning.
- Punishing first and asking questions later.
- Punishing a child for child-like behaviors such as clumsiness or being forgetful.
- Using punishment, both positive (adding something unpleasant) and negative punishment (taking away something desirable).

There were many good times, but there was also a lot of screaming, crying, threats, and fear.

For those who commit, raising a child is the most important task of their lifetime. It takes a special kind of self-awareness to raise a good person. Once again, the key is empathy. A parent has to consider how their child, at that age, with their current development, is feeling. Depending on the child's age, they often do not have the vocabulary to express themselves. Still, a parent must provide the child with the tools to communicate their feelings. It starts with setting an example. Get children comfortable with expressing themselves the way you would want them to by demonstrating it:

Look, kiddo, I need you to know that I am sad about the vase you broke. It was a gift from my Nonna, who I miss very much. I know you did not do it on purpose, but I asked you not to run into the house. I wish you had listened to me because I would not be upset with you and still have my vase. Help me pick up the pieces.

A child that only experiences emotions as unbridled anger will grow up meeting every situation with it. Men are especially susceptible to this. They are socialized from birth to toughen up and not show any display of sadness, disappointment, shame, or grief. The one emotion shown to them was anger, regardless of the situation. Yes, screaming and destroying are satisfying briefly because you feel like you let it out. It is a tragic cycle that will continue until children are taught to express their emotions properly at the time rather than bottling them up for appearances.

Children are volatile little bombs of emotions. They are in a world where every problem feels like the end of the world because they have no frame of reference. They also don't have the capacity to recognize and communicate their emotions. They do what most adults do when they are at the end of their rope, they explode.

Father: Why are you so angry?

Daughter: I can't find my doll!!

Father: Oh no! Is that doll special?

Daughter: Yeah.

Father: Why is it so special?

Daughter: I can't sleep without it! I'm scared!

Father: Does the doll help you be brave?

Daughter: Yeah, she keeps me company in the dark.

Father: I get it. I used to sleep with a teddy bear when I was your age. You fell asleep on the couch last night so let's check there.

Daughter: Okay.

Father: See it was stuck between the cushions!

In the above example, instead of giving his daughter "something to cry about", the father took the time to understand why his daughter was upset. She wasn't throwing a tantrum for the hell of it; she was genuinely scared. He found an amicable solution and diffused his daughter's frustration. Reacting with anger at their symptoms does nothing for the child except tell them their emotions are a burden. They are robbed of the tools to deal with them, and the parent gets mad when their child can't manage their emotions and seeks other outlets.

Fostering empathy, emotional connection, rationalization, and self-esteem is the best way to raise a child to be able to communicate true emotions. Encouraging their hobbies is crucial. Sharing joys and interests should be the easy part. If they can't do that, how can they express their need for help with homework, or that they are getting picked on or are fighting with their friends? They will grow up self-assured, knowing how to communicate appropriately and instead of seeking approval, they know they have a parent who will always love them and listen to them.

Talking Your Way Through a Happily Wedded Life

Getting married is easy; staying married is a different beast entirely. Since Ronald Regan introduced *no-fault divorces* during his tenure as governor of California, it seems like divorce is in fashion. People now have the agency to leave unsatisfying or even hostile marriages. From a societal standpoint, this is a good thing, but divorce will still flip a person's life overnight in an instant.

When viewing content created by marriage counselors and jilted lovers, one common thread emerges, someone stops engaging. They assume everyone is on the same page; they are a family! The other person might be trying to highlight the issues, whether it's the loss of spark, intimacy, uneven division of labor, different philosophies around parenting, or the sudden realization that they are incompatible. Eventually, both parties break down, and they are no longer a united front. Instead, they are either competing or essentially roommates.

That wedding band creates such a false sense of security that frequently, people are surprised when getting served with divorce papers.

They'll get over it; they will never leave.

This mantra of denial will keep repeating in their heads until, one day, it stops being true. That relationship that started with so much promise fell apart, and they were too blind to see it. So, what are the secrets to a long marriage and a happy one? The first and most obvious part is being compatible in values. These core beliefs are rarely changed, and attempting to do so will only lead to resentment.

If a person is perfect, only one wants kids, and the other is firmly against it, then they are not perfect, are they? In the initial courting process, you cannot avoid those deep conversations out of fear that you are incompatible.

These are not Schrödinger's values[1]; the result isn't dependent on an observer; they are static. Just because you avoid the subject does not mean it goes away. Kids, religion, where you want to move, overall career goals, dynamics with the in-laws, and lifestyle choices are all things that need to be confronted early before you get too invested.

You should still talk to your partner like you are dating when you are old and gray. Giving compliments, wooing, laughing, and playing don't have an age restriction.

Every positive thing you do in the relationship is foreplay– John M Gottman

Your partner should always be exciting and challenging. Never stop seeking to empathize and understand. Are they just mad because you didn't put away your shoes or because they spent all day cleaning, and not only was it not acknowledged, but you also tracked dirt into the house and made no effort to maintain the home? Is your partner being a nag, or are you just getting defensive at their repeated attempts to make you aware there are issues?

We all change, so there is always something to discover about your life partner. Keep dating, and continue to

---

[1] Schrödinger won the physics Nobel Prize in 1933 for his discovery of new productive forms of atomic theory.

explore each other in the bedroom besides pumping and dumping. You should never be afraid to speak your mind on legitimate issues. That is the secret to a happy marriage.

Making Friends

When you are out and about, communication can be fun or terrifying, depending on your predisposition. Conversations always run the risk of going sour in a loud environment, in small groups, or on a date. We all want to make friends, but breaking down those communication and emotional barriers can be intimidating, especially if the group has a history. You can start something great when you meet new people; seize your moment.

Talking in Small Groups

Small group dynamics are funny, especially if you know the people. You see who has the more domineering personality of the group, the ones that have to prove something, and the more passive ones. You can leave one of these conversations dejected because you couldn't get a word in despite knowing these people. Unless an extrovert adopts you, you must make friends on your own, spend the night married to the snack table, or play with the dog (though this might be a win).

For one, organic group conversations tend to become saturated once more than four participants are introduced. This is called *the dinner party problem.* Once this limit is met, the conversation tends to splinter, or people become excluded (Krems & Wilkes, 2019). If you see a group that already has four people, it's best to leave them alone. If you see five, chances are one person is getting left out. Congratulations, you have found your mark.

Building rapport quickly is imperative. Introduce yourself and shake hands, (or a brief hug if appropriate) to allow brain chemistry work in your favor. Since you are in the same place, you already have common ground to start asking questions. Remember, you need to ask open-ended questions to have a good conversation. Asking yes or no questions can feel like an interrogation and will end the conversation abruptly. Since you are the fish out of the water, use that to your advantage and get the person talking about anything and everything.

Use all your tricks; be relaxed, take up space, and even if you don't know a single person there, conduct yourself like you have known everyone there for years. It's tempting to want to close yourself off when you don't know anyone, but you must resist the temptation to make yourself smaller or cross your arms. Remember you are confident and aren't scared of rejection (even though you are screaming on the inside).

Men are From Mars; Women Are From Venus

When making friends, men and women could not be more different; your strategy should change depending on your new friend. Generally, men tend to bond over activities and shared interests. Male bonding is born from overcoming challenges as a group, whether it's sports or occupational. There is a reason that the military (still very much male-dominated) is so much more fraternal than an office. Going through all those trials and tribulations with your squad builds strong bonds that members would die for each other. Fathers and sons go fishing, fraternities party, boy scouts camp, all bonding over shared goals and problem-solving. Men tend not to share many personal details to earn each other's trust.

Women, on the other hand, bond through face-to-face conversation. They get brunch, chat while getting their nails done, or just sit for coffee. The activity is the center for men and the backdrop for women's conversation. They catch up, gossip, commiserate, and have intensely vulnerable discussions. Women are even more likely to share intimate details about their sex life and health; most men find this inconceivable. Think about it: when men are so close, they start sharing their emotions and are in sync outside a male bonding activity, referred to as a *bromance*.

Collecting Role Models: The Wonderful Friendship of Turk and JD

If you have ever seen *Scrubs,* you would recognize the famous bromance of JD and Turk. They were colleagues at the fictional Sacred Heart Hospital, where JD was an internal medicine doctor and Turk was a surgeon. The thing is, they rarely worked directly together on cases and did not have similar hobbies. Turk was an athletic "man's man", while JD was more effeminate. When you think of most male friendships, you might fail to see why they are so close. Their bond came from sharing their emotions and insecurities and commiserating over their struggles in the medical field. They understood each other so well and genuinely loved each other. It is the type of friendship that anyone would be lucky to be a part of. Yet, on any other show, especially made during that time, having two men be so close would be the subject of ridicule or classify them as a romantic couple.

JD and Turk's ability to be vulnerable with each other, be patient, and challenge each other might look strange to some men, but if you attached those same qualities to female friendships, no one would bat an eye. While you might be saying that it's just how men are and they don't need to be vulnerable to be friends, ask yourself, is this working?

An increasing number of men feel isolated; they may have friends, but no one to express their emotions. Many boys lack mentoring from older men and have no idea how to grow into well-adjusted men in today's society. They may even turn to women in an attempt for emotional validation, but they end up scaring her away by dumping too much too quickly. If Turk and JD's friendship were seen as just a good male friendship instead of a bromance, maybe men would be better off.

How Our Roles in Society Hold Us Back

When dealing with the opposite gender, there is much pressure to try to become what we think they want. Men assume all women want strong manly men who will fight to the death for their honor, and women assume all men want demure, quiet princesses who are Cinderella by day and Marilyn Monroe in the sheets. It sounds absurd, but we tend to go to extremes when we get in our heads. If you are a more sensitive guy who can knit a killer sweater, you might feel lost in approaching women because you feel like you don't fit their ideal. Likewise, you might have scared men away if you were opinionated and confident. Since men and women are socialized so differently, they have no frame of reference as to what is going on in the other person's head, not to mention, as we established above, men and women bond differently.

It's easy to feel busted, but that can't be further from the truth. We are conditioned from birth to be sorted into boys and girls. We are given pink or blue before we even leave the womb. Parents have burned down acres of protected land for the sake of a gender reveal. Boys and girls have different expectations in behavior, have different toys to reinforce societal expectations (boys get nerf guns, girls get dolls), are pushed into different interests, and any deviation (especially for boys) is immediately stamped out.

The solution, though, is not being something you are not. Lean into your quirks and maybe work dates around them. Chatting over drinks is not the best way to introduce yourself to everyone. Instead, take a page out of the male bonding book and do an activity instead. Suppose you do not feel the need to identify as a manly lumberjack type. In that case, you can still demonstrate decisiveness and competence (still traditionally masculine traits) through an activity, especially if you are more familiar with the activity than the date.

As for women, remember men bond through action over words. You can show your date your ability to cooperate, support, and emotions (considered feminine traits) in a context that will make a man feel like he is a part of it. A weird fitness class, cooking class, or laser tag can do this. If you are more of a take-charge woman, you can also see how your date responds to not being in total control if you pick an activity with which you are more familiar. If they cannot stand being at a disadvantage, it's probably not going to be a good fit down the road.

Key Takeaways

- We wear different hats when we are in different places and learning to lean into that will make you an effective communicator.

- At work you should be friendly and open to conversation, but not necessarily a completely open book. Keeping coworkers at a distance is essential.

- Meetings are the worst but if you want to be a leader you need to learn to manage them. Setting expectations and enforcing a structured environment is key.

- Talking in small groups can be tricky thanks to the dinner party problem. As Krems & Wilkes suggest, odd numbered groups often have one person left out of the conversation entirely, so look to join a group of 5 rather than 4 to save yourself from being the third wheel.

- Bonding for men and women is born from different experiences. Men bond through activity, women bond through emotions.

- If you don't meet what you consider to be the standards of your given gender, don't fret. Leaning into those differences in a more suitable environment will allow you to be true to yourself while still impressing your date.

HOW TO BE THE BOSS
(AND NOT END UP HATED)

"Any man that says "I am the king" is no true king..."

- TYWIN LANNISTER

You have been honing your communication abilities and, surprisingly, yielded the results you wanted. You are now a department manager in a medium-sized tech company with a team of five people under you. For this exercise, let's say you got to pick your team, and everyone is good at their job.

You are also qualified because you are familiar with all aspects of the department though you might not be an expert in it. You have been set up for success, but it will only happen if you lead the team effectively. Let everyone know that you can handle being a leader, but it's another thing to have this group of people foisted upon you to guide you with real-world reputation and financial stakes. You are the captain now, so will you steer the ship into the sunset or an iceberg?

Acting Like a Leader

We have all experienced both good and not-so-good bosses. A boss can be bad for various reasons: they are incompetent, have no soft skills, are lazy, micromanage, are too aggressive, or are only looking out for themselves. Poor management can crush a dream job and destroy morale. It's not enough that you sign off on paychecks; the team has to respect you. People who look up to their superiors will want to excel not just because it's their job, but because they don't want to disappoint you. Long story short, it's not about how much you know or how tough you are, it's all about charisma.

With charisma, you don't need powerful connections, money, or expertise to have people follow you. People follow because you have this quality about you that is exciting and points to success. Tech-savvy people flounder in mid-tier roles because they lack the charisma to succeed in a group. You must make sure that people listen when you speak, follow your emotional cues, and do not question your judgment without good reason. You wield power through your actions, not by telling people that you have power.

It's About the Team

If you want to succeed in your new role, you need to communicate in a way that fosters trust and *group cohesion.* This is how well the group works together and is predicated on four things:

- Attraction; how much the individuals in the group like each other.

- Sense of belonging.

- Coordination; how willing the team is to work with each other to accomplish a task.

- Shared emotions; when the group is all on the same emotional wavelength about their current state.

Group cohesion in a professional setting is already fostered by having separate departments, tangible tasks, and rewards for completing those tasks. People may need more time to be ready to trust their projects to other people or be acclimated to interacting with others. Weekly team meetings that create a united front are an excellent way to get everyone together!

The team need to be comfortable enough to laugh together and constructively criticize someone. Not wanting to rock the boat can cause people to clam up, even if they see something legitimate that needs addressing. They think to themselves:

I'm probably wrong about this.

Someone else will catch it.

I don't want this person to be mad at me.

If you create an environment where bad news generates a reaction instead of action, minor issues can turn into fires. This starts with you, the boss. Do not resort to outward displays of emotion when an employee expresses a concern.

Hey boss, where can I find more kits?

Wait, what? I just ordered these; we can't have run out already. Are you sure you don't have any more?

I was just going to ask where you put the new lot.

Oh.

The ability to speak freely is essential for creating a welcoming professional relationship. If a person trusts that you will not react negatively to a question or criticism, they trust you will have their back if someone else in the group doesn't. If you are unapproachable or constantly negative, this gets exhausting and creates an environment where your employee would rather waste hours than trust you enough to ask a simple question.

Finally, there are shared emotions, and this is where your managerial skills will show cracks first. If one part of your team feels excellent about a decision while another does not, you have to ask yourself why. There is room for encouragement and hope, but insisting that nothing is wrong is a recipe for disaster.

I don't know how I am going to finish this! We have sent the edit five times, and the client keeps adding and cutting stuff. They keep emailing me, and I don't know what to do!

Don't worry; this is simple! We've dealt with demanding clients before. As long as we put our heads down and work, it will be okay.

This may seem encouraging, but it downplays the employee's frustrations and uses the cursed words:

This is simple.

If a competent team member is having trouble, then things are not so simple.

Let them know you see the situation for what it is, but they will all work together to overcome it.

I know you have been working hard on this project. This is a difficult client, and you have handled everything so well. I will communicate with the client from here on out if you would like? Just focus on the edits, and I will take care of the rest.

Don't just talk about numbers; talk about emotions, stress levels, and have people be candid with you individually. If you can sense an issue, but the employee is keeping it to themselves, you may need to try a tougher line of questioning. A person may want to scream from the rooftops, but if they sense a loophole in your questioning, they may shut down. You have to be direct. Instead of:

Everything is going smoothly in the project, right?

Try:

What kind of issues have you been having in meeting your deadlines?

This is known as a *presumptive question* and it cuts right through the crap because it gives the impression that you already know part of, if not the whole, story. In one sentence, the manager has conveyed that they understand that the employee is struggling, affecting the timeline of the entire project.

Talking the Talk

When you are in charge, you have to think about your vision for your team and lead them in that direction. Unfortunately, the old proverb goes, "power corrupts" or reveals what a person is. The second a worker bee is given a clipboard or an extra title, it might turn into a monster. Suddenly, the small work is beneath them, the team is at their beck and call, and the control goes to their heads. Luckily, if you are self-aware, you probably won't become the subject of someone else's therapy appointment. As a manager, you have more power than you think over the people under you, and you have to accept that.

Hmmm, I'm not familiar with that particular database, but Sarah is. Sarah, can you show Devin the ropes on this one and let me know if you have any problems?

People respect you if you are willing to admit that you don't know something, and more importantly, they will be candid with you if you assign them something they are unfamiliar with. If you start bullshitting, the rest of your team will follow.

Look, I know that the dinner rush was very stressful for everyone. But you all did a great job. We got all the food out and made some good money.

Just that bit of encouragement will make the team feel seen and like they busted their butts for a good reason. They will go to bed with a sense of accomplishment instead of looking at job boards in a rage. Best of all, it doesn't cost the company a cent!

Playing Bad Cop While Looking Like the Good Cop

Learning the art of constructive criticism is essential for any leader. You must nip problems in the bud before the results can be felt outside your sphere. Criticism is best received when it is internal over external (Adelman & Verkuyten, 2019). You are guaranteed to feel much more defensive if the issue is public. Calling someone out on their shortcomings is difficult, but if done correctly, it can be a vital tool for your team's improvement.

- Never make it personal.
- Be specific.

- Emphasize what they did right on top of what they did wrong (but avoid the sandwich).

- Do not be overly optimistic or downplay errors.

Let's say you put Emily, the new girl just out of college, on labeling tubes. When Mary went to pull the tubes for additional analysis, she found that she could not read a lot of the writing, and pertinent information was missing. Mary was able to fix it, but it took her half a day. As the boss, you need to address this as next time the experiment might not be salvageable. Let's look at some poor examples first:

Didn't you learn this in school?

Instead of framing it as a mistake that can be fixed, this issue is now with her character. If you give the employee the impression that you think they are stupid, that genie can never go back in the bottle. They will stagnate or look for the door.

When dealing with a new employee, and a young one at that, they often have no frame of reference regarding on the job treatment. They may think such treatment is normal, which is a disservice to the people under you. You have a responsibility to your employees to help them succeed in their present role, and establish a path for future performance.

It's not a big deal. Just do it better.

This is too vague. "Better" is subjective, and doesn't address the issue of information being missed. Criticism without a concrete method of fixing something, or at least describing the problem, is punishment. Graphic designers always get this feedback when clients tell them their work doesn't "pop" enough. What does "pop" mean? This criticism gives you the illusion of being proactive, but you are setting a person up for failure by not having concrete solutions or standards.

Downplaying the issue is also ill-advised. It was a big deal; it took hours of someone else's time to fix, and stressed everyone out. Mary may not want to trust Emily as much now. She may feel you prefer Emily to her, which can cause discontent amongst the team. While you are sparing Emily's feelings, you are also invalidating Mary's experience.

It's not a big deal to me, but Mary seemed upset.

Never pit your coworkers against each other. Even if Mary was upset, you do not need to vocalize her emotions. Emily may internalize that and be afraid to go to Mary even if her anger is justified. Likewise, Mary talked to you in confidence and may feel betrayed that you made it look like she was angrier than she was at Emily.

You are doing a great job so far; your handwriting is messy. Still, your technique is getting better.

This is the controversial compliment sandwich. Some insist on it because it makes critiques more palatable by surrounding them with good news. Thanks to the *serial position effect,* this technique is already doomed since people tend only to remember the beginning and end of an information dump. The middle is the last place you want to put something important. You start by addressing the facts and how you and the manager feel about what happened. Avoid too many "you" statements, as that can raise a person's hackles. When discussing solutions, go for "we" statements and end on a high note about how you are confident that you have given your employee the tools never to repeat that mistake and that you have also learned something from this.

Hey, I wanted to talk about the project. We need to address one thing, and we will be back on track. The labeling on the tubes caused some confusion; it took some time, but we were able to fix it. I want to emphasize how vital it is to clearly label the vials. Other people need to be able to read it months later. Write slowly, with a fine-tip pen, and ask yourself if what you have written can be mistaken for anything else.

I noticed 4's and 9's looked pretty similar. This cannot be rushed. I should have standardized our labeling methods since we are a new team and might have different ways of working. Let's decide what information should be included and defer to that. If anyone questions you about the time you are taking with this step, ask them to talk to me about it.

The situation was discussed clearly without pointing the finger, faults in the pipeline were addressed and corrected, and the manager let Emily know that he still valued her input.

Key Takeaways

- Becoming a leader and staying a leader requires you to trust your team.

- It's not about you or your ego anymore. By propping up the team, you elevate yourself.

- Your team also needs to trust that you have their best interests at heart.

- You cannot be nice all the time, which is why delivering effective criticism is essential.

- Criticism should be professional, actionable, delivered in plain sight, and should never throw other members of your team under the bus.

SHUT UP AND LISTEN!

"We have two ears and one mouth so that we can listen twice as much as we speak."

- EPICTETUS

Joshua is on his first date in a while. He decided to wait a while before jumping back in after his relationship of two years went sour. He felt out of practice, and frankly exhausted by the dating app experience. He finally got a match and was having fun talking to her. Joshua asked her out for coffee, and she said she was delighted to go.

Joshua sat in the coffee shop and greeted his stunning date. Suddenly, he was overcome with nerves.

Sadie: Hi, are you Joshua? I'm Sadie! Nice to meet you.

Joshua: (internally) Crap, she is way too pretty. What am I doing here? I'm not ready for this! Am I dressed suitable for this? I'm going to screw this up if I'm not careful F@*K, F@*K, F@*K!

...Yeah, I'm Josh from Tinder; thanks for coming by.

(internally) Thanks for coming by??? She is here on a date, not buying a candle!!!

Joshua had never felt this discombobulated when talking to someone else. He suddenly felt like he had something to lose if he was not otherwise perfect. They both ordered coffee, making small talk about the shop and the weather. It was a pitiful start in Joshua's mind, but Sadie seemed fine with it. After they sat down, Joshua was determined to salvage this less-than-stellar first impression.

Sadie: So Josh, while we were texting, you mentioned that you were still fairly new to this area. Has my lovely hometown been treating you well?

Joshua: ...uhhhhh yeah! I like it so far, how about you, how long have you been living here?

Sadie: Since it's my hometown...all my life, I moved out here for college, but I was raised here and have spent most of my adult life here.

Joshua: (internally) Dammit, that was a stupid question, Josh! The word 'hometown' should have been a clue!!

Oh right! Sorry, well, what was it like growing up here? It's a lot different than the farmlands I am accustomed to.

Sadie: I'm sure the space and fresh air were awesome growing up. This city is crowded and loud, but there's a lot to do here! I was able to walk everywhere as a kid and...

Joshua: (internally) She probably thinks I'm some country bumpkin, no, that's not fair she hasn't given you that impression, let's see, she's from the city, so I should ask her about her favorite restaurants and maybe hidden gems to keep the conversation going. I can't look stupid in front of her. She's got a master's degree, and I only have a bachelor's; she's cute and sweet; why is she wasting her time? This was a mistake, but maybe I have a shot. I just have to be normal for once!

Sadie: ...so Josh, how have you been spending your free time here? Or have you just been settling in before you paint the town red?

Joshua: Just settling in still, but I'd love some recommendations. What is your favorite place to eat?

Sadie: Oh, I could have sworn I just said Joe's Pizza since I was a kid.

Joshua: F@*K!

Knowing what to say and how to say it is only one part of becoming an effective communicator. our attention should be directed on what the other person is saying! Now you might be saying:

How dare you? I am a great listener! I am here to learn how to talk; how is this helping?!

Don't feel bad; most people are terrible at listening, which is doubly true if communicating takes a lot of effort. A person can't juggle two streams of consciousness at once. Have you ever been in the middle of two conversations? You cannot take in both of them at once, and you end up awkwardly interjecting in both conversations because you only end up with pieces of both stories. Talking and listening is the same way.

We get hung up on how we will package what we are saying, how we will come across, and how the other person will react that we are not internalizing what the other person is talking about. We may even start to forget that conversation is a two-way street and not realize that we are beginning to dominate the conversation, making the person a spectator when they should be a participant.

What is Listening?

What do we mean by "listening". We have been taught to listen since our parents decided we could understand phrases like "I love you" and "Don't stick the forks in the outlets!" However, we have all been guilty of times when we spaced out, misunderstood, or failed to read between the lines of a conversation. There are four types of listeners:

- Non-listeners
- Marginal listeners
- Evaluative listener
- Active listener

Non-listeners are at the bottom of the totem pole. They have no interest in what you are saying, will space out or interrupt. Long story short, they take in none of what you are saying.

Next is the marginal listener. These are the ones that hear the sounds coming out of your mouth but not much else. These types are half awake during a chemistry lecture, hearing concepts and familiar words but unable to apply them to anything; we have all had our moments. This can also be a personality trait of someone who is obtuse and lacks critical thinking skills.

Worker: Hey boss, the sequencer stopped.

Boss: ...okay.

Worker: Isn't there something we should do about it?

Boss: oh!

Then we have the evaluative listeners which is the last level that can be done passively. They try to listen but come up shy of absorbing intent and nuance.

Worker: Hey boss, my daughter is sick, and her daycare is calling.

Boss: I hope she feels better.

The next day...

Boss: Why did you leave early without telling me?

Worker: I told you my daughter was sick, and I had to get there.

Boss: That is not what you said!

Some people had the ability to learn to listen, never had to deal with language barriers, and chose to be this way. However, special consideration is needed if someone is neurodivergent or just learning a language. Those who are neurodivergent have trouble understanding sarcasm, tone, or intent, as they cannot recognize social cues.

I always think of the character Sheldon Cooper from *Big Bang Theory* here. He is a certified genius, but oblivious to social cues and sarcasm. Such individuals may internalize something that was initially meant as light teasing as legitimate criticism. People learning a new language, especially English, deal with convoluted spelling and grammar rules and have to contend with dialects, colloquialisms, and tonality. The 2001 movie *The Princess Diaries* sums this up nicely:

Mia: Shut up!

Queen Clarisse Renaldi: I beg your pardon, "Shut up"?

Consulate Maitre'D: Oh, your majesty, in America, it doesn't always mean to be quiet. Here it could mean, "Wow, gee whiz, golly wolly"...

It's not that the person is not listening; they legitimately don't have the tools to interpret the information. They will in the future, especially if you are patient with them and let them be comfortable enough to make mistakes in front of you.

Put in the Work and Become an Active Listener

Active listening takes patience and practice. Instead of just hearing the words, you need to comprehend and *remember* what the other person is saying. You need to be able to interpret how they are saying it, why they are saying it, their body language, and how they feel. It is a rare skill in this individualistic society, but that is why active listeners go far in this world.

There are five aspects to active listening:

- Not interrupting

- Maintaining interest

- Postponing evaluation

- Organizing information

- Showing interest (not the same thing as maintaining interest)

There are many reasons why people interrupt, and they are not all malicious. Some may be confused and will insist on clarification instantly. Some feel they have heard enough and can offer a solution. They think this is kindness, and even if their answer is sound, the person still feels cut off. You see this all the time in relationships. A woman comes home and wants to vent about getting passed over for a promotion. A man comes in, and mid-rant tells her how she should talk to the manager or quit and how he will support her. He is missing the point of why she is venting. She has thought of all these solutions already; she needs someone safe to release and validate this pent-up frustration. She is looking to bond emotionally with a person she trusts, not solve her problems.

Maintaining interest is not the fake head shaking or saying "yes", "okay", or "right" when you sense a conversation beat. This is taking a legitimate interest in what a person is saying. You are listening to the details and looking at the body language changes as details are presented, even if the person is talking about their stamp collection.

Being bored and not listening usually go hand in hand. Unfortunately, when we lose interest, we start to space out and start thinking about the fact we have to swing by the store to pick up more toilet paper or how we are ready to crawl into bed and read a book. You go into autopilot and start making sounds and gestures we associate with listening. Before we know what has happened, minutes have passed, and you have not heard a damn thing.

These are huge issues with the neurodivergent community. People with ADHD tend to have worse short-term memories; and will interrupt out of fear that they will forget. They are also impulsive, meaning they don't quite think through the consequences of interrupting. Some also feel natural pauses in conversation as an eternity and have to fill in the space. It makes for a difficult childhood as other children find this behavior annoying and will isolate them. People with ADHD can be overstimulated and anxious; they know they have to focus on what a person is saying. Still, they might become distracted by their worry that, before they know it, they have failed to take in any information.

To become an active listener, you must resist the urge to jump to a conclusion before a person is finished talking. Once you settle on a conclusion, you might have a bias toward the facts that justify your opinions. You have effectively stopped listening. What you say next will be based on half-baked information and ideas.

Now you have heard everything a person has to say. You must organize all that information on top of their physical cues and what you know about the person.

What has this person told me, what does this mean to them, how are they feeling, and what can I do?

If someone trusts you with something, there must be a reason for it. You might be close friends, a professional they trust, or they might see you in a way you did not realize. You need to look below the surface, read between the lines and formulate a response.

Finally, you have to show interest. People need to know you are internalizing what they are saying. The easiest way to do this is through mirroring. We have discussed this already but simply repeating what a person said helps a person feel heard and, more importantly, understood. If their tone is more sullen, speaking slowly and softly will help them to see that you understand the gravity of the situation. If a person sadly says:

My dad can't make it to my birthday this year.

Responding with,

WTF? That guy has a lot of nerve; I can't believe him!

This is not the best move, even if you think you are showing concern and empathy. The person might be bummed, but maybe they have made peace with it or understands that the situation is unavoidable. They can recognize that the father may be getting pulled into work and has no choice in the matter but still be sad about it. Your friend may now feel uncomfortable that you seem to view their father (a person they love) in an antagonistic light and may blame themselves, adding another layer of sadness.

Try to aim for:

My dad can't make it to my birthday this year.

Oh, I'm sorry to hear that. I know you were really excited to see him since it's been a while. Your dad always makes an effort to make it to your big days.

Yeah, but his team is pulling him into work on a massive project with a tight deadline; he was so upset when he told me.

That really sucks. I hope you can call him on your day. Tell you what, I'll be sure to document the whole thing so he won't miss out. I can also remind you to try and facetime him so he can sing happy birthday.

A lot of people try to break the tension with a joke or a quip. Humor is not the answer to everything. If someone is being serious, it is not the time to break out of the pop culture reference you just thought of. Coping with a sense of humor is valid, but it's not for everyone. Maybe with some time, your brand of healing will be appreciated, but in a vulnerable moment, a person is seeking safety, not a clown.

The secret ingredient in active listening is empathy. You are not examining how you would solve a problem or focusing on saying the right thing so YOU look good; you are responding to how the other person feels. Empathy is an evolved form of sympathy. When you think about it, sympathy is a superficial emotion despite being one of the most revered. It simply acknowledges how *you* feel something terrible has happened to someone *else*.

I am sorry for your loss; I know how you must feel.

There is also the dreaded "I understand what you are going through". This isn't malicious, but it can come off as shallow. It is easy to tell someone that you are special because you understand. Unless you offer vulnerability, action, or understanding in a way that does not put you in the center, it's just empty words. Empathy is born from looking at another person, their history, personality, actions, and words and reacting with your own words and actions.

I am so sorry for the loss of your mother. She was a great woman, and I know the both of you were close. You leaned on each other so much; I can't imagine how you feel now. I know nothing I can say will make it easier, but when my dad died, I took it really hard, and many things got away from me. I will supply dinner for you and the rest of the family tomorrow. Give yourself a break.

That would be wonderful, thank you.

This person has been practicing active listening. They realize the whole situation instead of just how upsetting it is that their friend is sad. They understand their friend has lost a significant support system and is grieving. They mention that they have experienced this pain, but instead of that being the only indicator that they understand, they used that knowledge to anticipate a need and freely offered help.

Active Listening Is One of Life's Cheat Codes

Active listening is a quality that will get you far in life. For example, if you see your boyfriend has cologne samples in his hands, ask him about it. They may tell you they loved the scent but could not justify its price. The boyfriend will probably forget about this conversation, but the girlfriend won't. Three months later, the boyfriend celebrates a job promotion, and the girlfriend gives him the cologne he left behind. She tapped into something he probably did not even know he wanted until now. He sees the cologne as a symbol of his hard work, new status, and how his girlfriend always seems to read his mind. Active listening also makes you a much better problem solver because you have all the facts, even those not directly presented. You add humanity to a decision instead of something that is just pragmatic.

By actively listening, you see the entire person instead of parts of the whole. You get to know their interests, opinions, and quirks. You can only do this by not interjecting midway about how you have a negative view of something they like or how something they do is weird. A person will never trust you that way. It can be endearing watching another person explain their passion, even if you don't completely understand it. But you persevere, ask questions, and reflect an interest in this topic because it is important to them.

For example, let's say someone you are on a date with is passionate about pottery. They describe the process, the victories, and the challenges, such as how physically taxing it is and the frustrations when their pot flops over. By not interrupting their account or changing the subject to a topic you are more comfortable with, you demonstrate:

- You are secure enough not to need to have the upper hand in a conversation.

- You are genuinely interested in learning more about the topic.

- You are a person with whom they can feel safe discussing their passions.

- They are important and what they say matters.

Those qualities make you more desirable to a person because it shows them that you see them as an equal. Thanks to the rule of reciprocity, they will also be willing to hear you dump information on your passions. The next date comes up, and she says her back kind of hurts; you can ask if it was thanks to the work she has been putting into the pottery studio since she mentioned that it is a physically stressful hobby.

Even if the answer is no, she will feel good that you listened to the conversation and that she might have gone home and kicked herself over since they feared they bored you. You didn't just get this person to like you; you got them to trust you.

Key Takeaways

- Not all listening is created equal; active listening is what turns normal people into great communicators.

- You receive the nuance, emotion, and intent of the message with active listening, allowing you to pick up on more information than the person talking thinks they are letting on.

- Active listening allows you to connect with others, because they are giving you the answer on how to accomplish this.

- You can use active listening to your advantage by paying attention to what people desire and being the one to give it to them.

SELL YOURSELF LIKE A CHAMP

"If you're committed enough, you can make any story work. I once convinced a woman I was Kevin Costner, and it worked because I believed it!"

- SAUL GOODMAN

You need to be able to sell ideas and yourself if you want to have any agency in your life. Unfortunately, we see marketing as a dirty concept. Having to negotiate instead of being earnest with our intentions sounds cynical and fake. After all, the truth should be enough without any spin. Wrong! You may not believe you are the absolute best candidate for a job, but you sell yourself like you are since it is beneficial for you not to starve to death under a bridge. You are not thinking of what is best for the company, and why should you? The first thing to get out of your head is that selling means you have to be dishonest. You know how to present yourself in a way that is honest but also fits into the needed mold. This is crucial because you have to believe your hype. Any doubt will show in your body language and voice that will be picked up on right away.

Why are you the best person for this role?

Ummm...well, let's see, I am a full stack developer, and I can help maintain your app...so yeah, I think I am a good fit.

Vs

I am a full-stack developer with years of experience under my belt already. I have manned my projects, but your pipeline and methods are pretty similar to my last job. Training should be relatively quick, so I can integrate myself into your existing projects and already have ideas on new applications and improvements.

The first example shows a lot of doubt, the "I think" and "probably" are the only phrases that introduce doubt. There is also the lack of luster pitch; despite having the same qualifications, the first person only addressed something the interviewer already knew—that they could help. Of course, the interviewer knows that you would not be interviewing if that was not the case. The second example was a lot more self-assured. The interviewee did not sound like he thought he was qualified; he knew he was. They framed how the company will tangibly benefit from hiring them and included future plans telegraphing that they are creative and plan to be there for the long haul.

You need to be aware of several pieces to the sales pie: your audience, your pitch, and yourself.

Collecting Role Models: Pick a President!

While plenty of salespeople are thriving off the backs of their charm and brains, no other set of people demonstrated salesmanship better than anyone who has had to win a United States election. Despite their politics, one indisputable fact is that all forty-six of these men knew how to work the country for voters to put their trust in them as leaders of the free world. Elections changed forever in 1960, when they televised the debates between John F Kennedy and Richard Nixon. Both were equally matched in knowing how to talk to their base but had to adapt to this level of transparency. On television, Kennedy looked radiant, used the makeup provided to him, had a snappy haircut, and just looked presidential.

On the other hand, Nixon refused makeup, picked a suit color that blended into the background, and, between copious amounts of sweat and the five o'clock shadow, looked like he was struggling not to turn into a werewolf. Kennedy considered what the country would think of hearing and seeing the debate. It's why he won.

As cynical as this sounds, the campaign trail is filled with sales tactics used everywhere, from marketing life insurance to mattresses. Successful candidates always think of zingers and catchphrases to have their audience repeat them. Obama said, "Yes, we can!" Trump had "Lock her up", and many candidates defaulted to "USA, USA". That simple act of leading a crowd to repeat a simple phrase is electrifying. It is crowd psychology that can make anyone seem more charismatic.

With their appearance immaculate and their messaging cemented, a candidate must do one thing: dazzle the American people. Like any other salesmen, they know how to recognize America's pain points and sell them on a solution. Carter had a country traumatized by the Vietnam war, Regan knew that America was sick of the communist threat, and Clinton saw a financially strained America. Bush Jr saw an America still grappling with the war on terror. Obama had a country that had been through a conga line of economic upsets and war.

They all successfully tailored their message to the versions of America they were dealing with. You will notice that many speeches are quite vague so that the listener can insert themselves into the messages. When a person hears "tough times" they can insert the foreclosure of their mortgage, delayed retirement, a death in their family, or an illness. This is much more effective than going through a list of specific issues, so you hit everyone.

Presidents don't just sell themselves as an answer to a specific solution; they need to be THE answer. Their branding, repetition, generalized language, and charm make them accessible to anyone from rural Alabama to New York City.

Holding A Captive Audience

We all want things and need things. Selling a need is easy, once you can spot it. An example would be selling umbrellas as soon as there is a downpour. There is no skill, just opportunity. While this is a sure way to get paid, opportunity is sporadic; you need control in your business. The key to capitalism is the human nature of want. We have a thing, but we covet our neighbor's bigger, shinier possessions.

However, wants are considered frivolous; people tend to talk themselves out of luxuries or risks. Your target audience will not stay if you are not convincing. Right now, you are a nobody, interrupting their errands to give them an annoying pitch. You are easy to ignore or swat away, and that needs to change. You need to look, talk and behave like someone worth listening to.

Mirroring a pleasant version of your customer is a good start. It builds trust and gets them to like you on a subconscious level. You want your language to be competent but approachable. If you are selling a class, odds are your target audience will only have a passing knowledge of the subject. You want to use simple language, avoiding jargon and long-winded explanations but at the same time you don't want to be condescending.

Say you came across a person selling their investment consulting service; which opening line would make you want to spend another second with this person:

Marketer 1: Oh man, you look broke; we can help you with that!

Marketer 2: This is a bear market; it is the ideal time to average down on some blue chips. When we enter a bull market, you will pay serious dividends even if you want to go short[2]. You can look into index funds and ETFs if you want to go long. What do you think?

Marketer 3: I can help grow your money for the future. Prices are low, so it's a rare opportunity to invest, and when the market recovers, you will profit. Are you looking for long or short-term gains?

The first was way too casual with the customer's pain point. While that pain is undoubtedly good motivation, the customer needs to know that you think there is hope that they can rise above it.

The second pitch focused on making the customer think the salesman knew what he was talking about. While it is reassuring, making the customer feel small and confused should not be the goal, especially if you want to target a broad audience. This can be forgiven if you want to target a small, niche, knowledgeable audience, but you will severely limit your prospective client pool because you cannot draw in new customers. The crypto and finance market is rife with this issue. Media and content produced by these types include technical jargon, lingo,

---

[2] Bear and bull markets are trading terms. A bear market occurs when securities fall, while a bull market is where securities rise for a sustained period of time.

and tons of acronyms and inside jokes. You can lose control of this club house mentality. While it is good to get customers to feel like they are a part of something, it can limit your reach when you try and tap into new markets. As a result, certain spaces, such as the PC community, gaming, and cryptocurrency, are noticeably devoid of women.

The Art of Storytelling

Picture this: you are selling a service. How would you go about it? You might say your strategy depends on the type of service, right? WRONG! Let's say you are selling a coding course. There are dozens out there, and some are free. Since you are just starting and have expenses associated with the course, you cannot afford to give it away. You might be tempted to try the following:

Thirty hours of lectures and interactive lessons for each language.

Instructors from Cornell University.

Pick from ten programming languages.

This pitch lacks empathy. You are selling why YOU think the course is great. These are enticing facts, but it's not enough to get someone to part with their hard-earned money. Let's say you pivot to describing why a person might want this:

Fun and interactive learning style from professionals in the industry.

We will teach you everything you need to know.

Build simple tools to make your life easier.

These are slightly better, but still not enough. Your pitch should never include the words "I" or "we", the customer needs to be the star. Wants are a fundamental human weakness, but people are aware of this. You need to figure out what your customer wants and then frame that as a need. It is not just a course that will teach them Python or Java; purchasing this might change their lives. Ask yourself:

A person would want this thing because they need _____

That need is where the money is. While a person may not need a programming course, their desire in wanting to learn to code might be rooted in a more significant need (or at least a more powerful want):

Earn more money in tech by learning how to code.

Have the tools to build your apps and businesses.

Learn how to make money from the comfort of your home.

Learn on your own time with our flexible schedule.

You are barely selling the course at this point. A potential customer is weaving a story in their head about how their life will change for the better with a simple purchase. You should look at how you have been successfully socially engineered to buy or sign up for things. The ads specifically targeted homemakers that were, unfortunately, feeling unfulfilled and lonely. These groups have built communities, hierarchies, and perks. The only reality is buying the rights to sell cheap leggings or dietary supplements that taste like aquarium gravel, customers thought they were buying one dream: to find a way to a life of luxury easily. It's a common fantasy we all have, but when you say it so nakedly, it sounds dumb. That's why you package it into something that looks attainable. You don't buy a gym membership; you are purchasing the key to losing weight, looking and feeling better; you don't buy a meal prep service; you buy time that would save you and not feel the effects of constant fast food. The list goes on and on.

Donning a Persona

To her friends, Camilla was lame (but that's what made her endearing). She dressed modestly; for the most part, she was going to school to be a pharmacist, crocheted her scarves, and never really dated. She was a reserved girl next door who barely drank, let alone went to clubs. That is why everyone was gobsmacked when she said she had just got a new job as a bottle girl in one of the busiest nightclubs in the city. Everyone pondered how this quiet nerd would survive in such an environment. Camilla wasn't worried, though, because she had a strategy.

When getting ready for work, Camilla hyped herself with music and dance. She put on her skimpy uniform, which was nothing more than a sports bra and booty shorts, went full glam on her makeup, and styled her hair. By the time she was done, she was unrecognizable, and that was the point. She entered the building, greeting the security guards, manager, and fellow girls in a sweet yet more confident tone. When the lights went down and the music went up, that's when the transformation was completed.

Camilla tapped into that part of herself that she knows exists but can be exhausting to maintain. But she knew she would need to embrace this side if she wanted to make money. While she was not a natural flirt or a supermodel, Camilla walked and talked like she was. She held herself like the men at her table were lucky to have her there. While she never really danced with her friends, she danced across the floor and with her customers, knowing that she was there to make her customers feel like royalty.

After a night of pounding music, dancing, laughing, and light flirting with a dash of light arm touches, Camilla walked out with a grand in tips. She was exhausted and had no energy to talk to anyone the next day. Having this persona helped Camilla shift into the person she did not know she had in her to adapt. It also helped fit her into a club scene where her usual self probably would not have fit in, let alone make money. Her alter ego could do anything without feeling suffocated by Camilla's expectations of herself.

You might say, "I don't need this, I don't work with others, and even if I did, I hate selling". Some people are born salespeople; they can read people on the fly and say just the right thing to get them to buy into whatever they sell. The answer might be to don a persona that will help you get out of your way. This is much easier when you know your contact with the person is limited since they have no frame of reference. Use neuro linguistic programming to model yourself from the greats, and with enough practice, these traits will become a part of you, not something you have borrowed. Be open to changing your strategy and style to align with your inspiration.

For an interview or a first date, you want to don a persona that is sustainable but still insanely charming. It all starts with body language and face. Look confident and relaxed. Have specific rules and positions you can default to convey how at ease you are. Lean forward slightly when someone talks, look them in the eyes even if it is difficult (or at least their forehead), and don't be afraid to take up space. Congratulations, you have donned the "I belong here, and I am happy about it" persona, even if you are a gigantic ball of nerves. It's not about being dishonest or fake. We all have different ways of carrying ourselves; the sooner we acknowledge this fact, the sooner we can use it to our advantage.

Having the tools to deal with people and situations we don't like is a part of succeeding. Exploring that part of yourself is a blessing, even if you treat it as a separate entity in a consequence-free environment. Our typical personalities may not be equipped to deal with it, but there is a rockstar somewhere, just waiting to come out.

Key Takeaways

- When you sell you need to take yourself completely out of the equation and focus on the customer.

- People buy with emotion, so by reframing a want as a need so people are more compelled to spend money.

- Donning a persona might help you out when you need to turn up the dial in personality.

BEYOND THE BLACK MIRROR

"Conversation is king. Content is just something to talk about"

- CORY DOCTOROW

We have been talking about communication styles when dealing with flesh and blood people. Unfortunately, a lot of communication now is done through mobile devices. There is no room for ambiguity, assumptions, or redundancies. Communicating in the digital age is the same way. We cannot rely on tone, timing, or our intentions to deliver a message. Any miscommunication can lead to mistakes, delays, and a damaged reputation.

There are two worlds in digital communication, the professional and the personal. You would never text a date the same way you send a work email. A level of etiquette and bias will completely skew how someone takes a message depending on someone's position in the corporate hierarchy and even gender.

You've Got Mail!

Bart: But your ad says 'no money down.'

Shows an ad that says 'Works on contingency no money down!

Lionel Hutz changes the ad to read: Works on contingency? No, money down!

—The Simpsons

Sending emails is a deceptively stressful event where the slip of your finger can lead to disaster. Have you ever sent an email saying:

Thanks?

Instead of

Thanks!

It makes you want to crawl into a hole, knowing your incompetence is forever cemented in the digital realm. Every keystroke is subject to scrutiny, and you don't have tone, inflections, or context to support your point. It has to all be there in black and white.

Keep it Brief

You run the risk of more errors and confusion the more information you try to pack in. People are busy, they will not read an email that looks like a transcription of *Grapes of Wrath*. If something is crucial, it should be its single email. Emails for exchanging ideas should be treated like any other professional conversation, brief and to the point. Use formatting options such as highlights and bullet points to emphasize what is essential quickly. If the details are complex or if you run the risk of creating multiple conversation branches, it might be best to have a meeting instead.

Slow down!

Have you ever sent an email in the heat of the moment and had it blow up in your face? Despite being simpler on the surface, there is a ton of odd etiquette that goes with email and tons of things can be misconstrued as aggression. It's about reframing to get what you want without the other person knowing it. Say you need to check up on the status of an order. You might be tempted to write:

Where is this package? I thought you ordered it last week.

Despite being pretty neutral when spoken out loud, this email would either make someone's stomach drop or annoy someone because it can be seen as accusatory. Instead, slow down and reframe it as offering help even though all you need is information:

I noticed this package hasn't arrived. It's time-sensitive. Is there something you need from me so we can expedite this process?

This email is much easier to respond to because you (appear) to offer a solution and frame the problem as potentially your fault. Even if there is nothing you can do, just look like you are ready to make their life easier, and they are more likely to help you in turn thanks to the law of reciprocity. You have to spell these things out in emails since people's ability to discern an entire situation seems to go out the window in text form.

Be Thorough

Does this go against the "Be Brief" section? A little, but there is a method to the madness. You cannot leave room for ambiguity or error in an email. If you want someone to respond, write, *please respond.* If you are setting up an appointment, don't just include the date and time; include what day of the week it is and if it refers to AM or PM. You cannot assume anything, it is unfair to both of you, and just a few little bits of information can save you all a headache.

Thoroughness applies to responding to an email as well. Type out what you think the instructions mean, the ideal result, and the time frame established. That way, you have solidified the instructions twice (in case things change without your knowledge) and left no ambiguity about how you understood the message.

Never Email While Angry

While firing off a snappy email will show everyone you mean business, it's not the best idea. Emails are an incredibly sanitized method of communication. Expressing frustration is so roundabout it is comical.

- Per my last email → Can you read?

- There seems to be a breakdown in communication → How can you still not read?

- Going forward → You f#@ked up.

- Please correct me if I am wrong → I am giving you one chance to save face.

- Can I get an update on this → This better be done by the end of the day, or I'll kill your family.

Women face an even more uphill battle. In an attempt to avoid being misunderstood as "difficult" their email style is so sweet reading it will give you a cavity. There is a much more liberal use of exclamation points, so you know she is excited and happy. They tend to preface their thoughts with qualifiers that show doubt.

- I feel...

- If I recall correctly...

- I could be wrong, but...

Being wrong is one thing; wrong and confident is the kiss of death. As such, women will draft emails to lower expectations right from the start.

With all the etiquette involved in writing emails, you can see why rushing one in the heat of the moment invites disaster. One grammatical error or mildly snarky comment is magnified. An easy way to combat this is to write the receiving address after you write the message. It gives you time to digest what you just wrote out before you can never take it back.

Social Media

One of the most significant changes in modern society is our adoption of social media. A good social media game creates brand awareness, allows you to advertise in a way that is more palatable to the masses, including the ever elusive young people. Companies like Duolingo and ScrubDaddy have Tik Tok accounts cashing in on the latest trends that can tailor their brand identity in real-time. Individuals use social media to curate an idealized version of themselves. It can be a powerful way to shift people's expectations of you. Showcasing your talents, best beach body photos, and every success is seemingly mandatory in today's world like we all have something to prove.

Social Media also has the potential to completely blow up your life if you don't use it properly. These days people are a bit too comfortable online. We seem to have forgotten the lesson of "the internet is forever" and, as a society, circled back to posting every thought that comes into our heads. While celebrities are immune to cancellation, your average Joe is not.

By now, we have all seen a story about people getting fired over their TikTok videos. This is especially endemic in the medical field. Professionals who think they are being quirky will make a video in ten minutes and get themselves fired by lunch. Nurses on the clock, film themselves complaining about their job at the expense of those in their care and their families.

People caught up in a social media blunder might have just been trying to let off steam, but their actions just eroded the reputation of their employer. It is easier for a company to fire you than to weather the PR nightmare. If someone puts a phone in your face and asks you to say anything short of praising your work, say no.

We all have the right to our private lives or a side hustle; sometimes, social media is part of that. You need to learn how to protect yourself. Hiring managers will type in your name and see what pops up. If it is a shirtless picture of you on Instagram shotgunning a can of Bud Light, don't be surprised if you don't get a callback.

Every so often, google your name and see what pops up. You might catch your embarrassing live journal, a now tasteless joke you made on Twitter in 2009, or your old Facebook posts about how misunderstood you are.

If you want to have fun on social media, make one account that is your "public" account and keep that one squeaky clean, then under a pseudonym and new email make another account with the fun stuff. Make this profile private if you can (if you are running a business, this can severely impact how many eyes go on your page).

All of this gives you plausible deniability. Fair warning, background check software is getting wiser to the digital footprint. In the future, staying anonymous will be more challenging. You might be better off just being extra judicious about what you put into the world.

Virtual Meetings

The COVID-19 pandemic in 2020 flipped our entire society on its head. The rise of virtual work and meetings was a consequence that showed no signs of going away, thanks to its convenience. Entire businesses are being run from the comfort of home, which has been liberating for some. For others, it is a nightmare. Poor connections, lousy sound quality, and environmental distractions make navigating this new world overwhelming. If you thought reading people was difficult in person, adding the barrier of a screen is even worse.

You need to manage your first impressions on a webcam. It is difficult for someone to get a sense of you when you are static in your home. The mental effects of online meetings depend on the person:

- Since you are in your own home, you might be inappropriately relaxed in speaking and presenting yourself.

- You freak out because meetings are no longer spontaneous or small. The fact that you have to schedule and accept the invitation makes every little correspondence seem like an event.

If most of your meetings are done virtually, you have to set up your area so you don't look like you haven't slept in a week. No one looks as good on camera as they do in person. Bad lighting and worse angles can make you look downright cranky. You need to create the illusion that you are talking right across the table from the other participant. Make sure the camera is pointed directly at you, not from a downward angle. Don't sit so close to it either; you wouldn't invade someone's personal space like this in person, would you?

Prop your laptop up on a stand or a pile of books, and sit back. Put away the dirty dishes, hide that pile of laundry and throw out the take-out boxes. If you run out of time, blur your background. If you are on camera a lot, it might be time to invest in some decent lighting. Overhead lights, especially with yellow bulbs, can be unpleasant and wash you out. Ring lights are not just for influencers and web streamers. They are a cheap and easy way to always look good on camera.

Try and make the environment as quiet as possible for the meeting. especially if there's noise in the background such as a dog continuously barking, or a crying baby being picked up by your microphone. It is unfair to everyone involved if you don't at least mute your microphone when you are not talking. Just because you have gotten used to it does not mean that others are.

The barrier of a screen impacts the rules of body language. Suddenly you are not feeding off the energy of a flesh and blood person; you are staring at either the entire group on the screen or the unforgiving void of the camera.

Unfortunately, you have to train yourself to look at the camera, even though human nature will fight us on this one. Looking at the screen will result in you looking off to the side, which may make the people on the receiving end not feel as invested in the content. It's like being in school; you don't break out your phone while making eye contact with the teacher.

This is challenging because you need to monitor the audience to gauge reactions. One distraction you can minimize is yourself. If you find yourself staring at your view-finder, turn that off. It's natural to feel uncomfortable on camera, especially speaking. The last thing you need is to be reminded of that fact on the screen.

Key Takeaways

- There are a lot of adjustments to be made if you are speaking online rather than in person.

- Emails are fickle things, you should never send one haphazardly.

- Social media is ubiquitous but dangerous if you do not use it right. Either keep it clean or create separate accounts.

- Never disparage your employer, customers or patients in social media, even if you think it's funny. Free speech does not apply, and you will get fired.

SINGLE AND READY TO MINGLE

"Charm is more valuable than beauty. You can resist beauty, but you can't resist charm."

- AUDREY TAUTOU

There is no other mode of communication more confusing, labyrinthine, and demoralizing than modern dating apps. It is also the most popular way to meet someone nowadays, so if you want to increase your chances of going on a date, you must know how to use them.

There are a few pros to dating apps. You have access to thousands of faces on your phone. Not having to go out and spend your hard earned cash just for a chance to talk to another person is a plus. With dating apps, you can meet someone from the comfort of your bed and start a conversation...right?

Modern dating is both frustrating and dehumanizing. Every other profile is either a bot, scammer, or catfish. You can only provide a keyhole view into your life with limiting prompts and photos. Dating apps are picture-based first and foremost, so if you are not photogenic, you are discarded to the left swipe cemetery. If you make a connection, the overwhelming number of options causes people to ghost without warning.

While apps are complicated for everyone, men seem to get it the worst (at least initially). They need to stand out, but their chances are also hurt by how others on the app behave.

- Men far outweigh women on these apps, so women have an overwhelming number of choices, though this dilutes the quality of those matches. As a result, men cannot afford to be sloppy. You will be taken as you are so present yourself as someone that someone would want to date.

- Men make it harder for other men. A bad interaction with a man, whether they sent the woman an unsolicited nude, dehumanizing, or catfished (yes, men catfish as well), chases women off apps, making the pool even smaller.

- Men's swiping strategies destroy the dating app system. Out of desperation, men will right-swipe every woman and determine if they want to interact later. This inflates the number of matches on the woman's side and buries sincerely interested matches. A woman may only collect a handful of matches so they don't have to juggle many conversations at once. The rest will be at the bottom of the deck or never be opened. Women get excited about their matches, only to become frustrated when the guy never responds. It's classic game theory, and men only hurt themselves with a shotgun approach.

- Your first picture is everything; a bad first picture will send you to the shadow realm without a girl even scrolling down.

- You have to be honest without putting a spotlight on your flaws. It is a delicate balance that can leave someone feeling deceived if not met.

- Your ability to have a conversation will be on full display in the texting stage. You cannot hide behind your tone or use your face. It is on you to make your intentions clear. Humor is something you must be very careful with jokes, lose timing, and delivery behind the text.

The Story of One-Hundred Swipes

Name: Monica D'Angelo

Age: 28

Education: Graduate Degree

Occupation: Scientist at Biotech Company

Height: 5'2"

Location: New York City

Bio: Looking for the Gomez to my Morticia!

When I'm not tending to my cell cultures, I enjoy exploring wine bars, going to live shows, taking the occasional painting class, and working out. If I like you a lot, I just might cook you something! If you want to go out and nerd together, drop a line :).

Best travel story: I almost got eaten by a shark while surfing in Hawaii.

I nerd out on: Cooking! I love the history, culture, and technique of it all. Currently, I'm perfecting my blueberry cheesecake recipe. I need someone to eat my experiments with!

My favorite qualities in a person are: Kindness and curiosity.

Monica uses her precious break time at work to swipe on dating apps. She is hoping for a relationship but is not opposed to some mutually respectful fun along the way. After all, it's about the journey, not the destination. She is no model, but she takes pride in her appearance. Her hair is neat, her makeup is subtle but flattering, and she works out three times a week. She chose her photos to try and give men the best idea about what she was like. It was challenging to reduce her life to this, but she thinks she managed well enough.

1. A once-in-a-lifetime shot at the botanical gardens. The lighting is perfect, her hair and makeup are on point, and she is smiling brightly. She is entirely unobscured by sunglasses or a large hat, and her whole body is visible. It is the type of photo that men would find attractive yet attainable.

2. Monica was a bridesmaid at her sister's wedding.

3. Monica is surfing; she is in a swimsuit and is all smiles.

4. An adorable baking picture where Monica is covered in flour but proudly holds a cake.

5. Monica poses with her friends at Comic-Con.

She would describe herself as cute more than hot, but Monica is alright with that. She feels like she is in a place where she is secure enough to look for something serious. Overall, she is your average big city woman in her late 20s with her life together; she has a good job, lives independently in a decent apartment, has friends, and has hobbies. She even has a savings account! Now she is just looking for someone to share that life with.

Monica does not have a particular type. She is petite, so she does not need anyone tall. She does not hold any man to a standard she cannot meet. All she wants is someone who similarly has his life together, who she is sexually attracted to and who she can mesh with personality-wise. Being active is essential, so Monica would want someone who can go on a five-mile run with her, spot her while she lifts and go on the occasional hike upstate.

That shouldn't be too difficult... right?

Tripping at the starting line-the first picture

Monica is shocked at the number of profiles that immediately turned her off before the word "go". Forty men were discarded based on their first picture alone. Before her brain registered what she did not like, instinct took over, and forty profiles were not even open. Everything she needed to know about the person was displayed and subject to rejection. What were some of these turn-offs, you might ask?

- Blowing smoke in the picture.
- Clothes not fitting or dirty.
- Flashing money.
- Posing with a car.
- Face obscured with a mask or bad lighting.
- Filters.
- Scowling.
- Camera points up at the person.

- Political paraphernalia.
- Posing with a woman and no other guy friends.
- Blurry photo.
- Holding a gun or any other weapon.
- Posing with a dead animal.
- Vacant stare.
- Strained smile.
- Mirror selfie with the toilet in the background.
- Taking a picture of nothing but their torso.
- Messy bedroom in the background.
- Joker cosplay.
- Wedding ring.

Are all of these fair?

Probably not. But it shows how vital the first picture can be. If the brain recognizes something it does not like or is associated with a bad memory, it'll tell your finger to swipe left and ask questions never.

Bios

Once Monica sees potential in the first picture, she scrolls down to the bio to see what makes these guys tick. Immediately ten are discarded because they are blank or just have a social media handle. The bio section of a dating app is begging for a bit of fun or creativity. Something that would make someone stand out among a sea of faces. Instead, it has become rife with repetitive cliches.

About me:

- Just ask.

- Looking for the Pam to my Jim.

- Mentions loving tacos or pizza.

- I'm not good at these.

Then there are the red flags that appear in a bio. Being overly negative in a bio is a dating cardinal sin. Whether it's about an ex or declining mental health, it's not a good idea to show a person that these qualities are so important that they are how you introduce yourself. The ex is self-explanatory. Mental health is a delicate topic. Many people suffer from mental health troubles, and more young people are medicated than ever. Still, if you met someone at a bar, would you introduce yourself with

My name is Ashley, and I have crippling anxiety.

Probably not. The person on the other side probably knows they are not equipped to deal with the subject matter in the bio and swipe left. Not to mention, plenty of con artists or entrepreneurs frequent these apps looking for an easy mark. Do not telegraph your vulnerability to strangers.

A second red flag is making a checklist of what you want in a person or, worse, a list of what you don't. Everyone is allowed to have preferences, but announcing makes you appear entitled and arrogant, depending on what you are asking for.

This can look like:

- Must be 6 feet or over!

- No tattoos!

- If you don't make six figures, don't bother.

- No fatties!

- Must be intelligent.

- No single moms.

- Looking for a feminine girl.

- No fake girls.

- No drama.

- Must be able to hold a conversation!

- No cheaters!

There is nothing wrong with having preferences, even strict ones, but most of this information can be deciphered from the profile. All you do is weed out someone who could be a great match because you alienated them with your negativity, even if they match all your preferences. A guy might not have any tattoos, but maybe his sibling is heavily tattooed; you just left a bad taste in his mouth. These are also signs of projection and insecurity. Someone who seems so incapable of having a conversation that they have to put it in their bio...is also the common denominator in all those failed contacts.

The exceptions are personality traits you like in a person or a hard redline for you or other people, such as a preference not wanting kids or a particular lifestyle where compromise is difficult. This is also where you put down if you have less conventional aspirations in dating, namely if you are ethically non monogamous, if you are in an open relationship or if you are looking for that elusive unicorn to spice up your love life.

Think of it from the other person's perspective, they have just matched with someone they find attractive, and you both get to chatting. You hit it off; you have compatible senses of humor, and just gel. And then, after an hour, you hit them with the prospect that they are, statistically speaking, most likely wholly romantically incompatible. Sitting on this information will never make it better; either the other person is open to the idea or they aren't.

All you have done is waste this person's time and emotional bandwidth. Yes, it will lower the number of matches you get, but the ones that do match will be more compatible off the bat.

Of the fifty that made it to this round, thirty were discarded due to the above behavior or blatant red flags such as sexualization, and fetishization. That left twenty men who had compelling pictures and bios.

The Whole Package

Some profiles look good at first, but it tends to fall apart once you see the whole picture. One common mistake is making your photos all too similar. The same clothes, pose, and smile can all make a profile, and therefore a person look boring. Another error has a group picture as the first image. It's annoying to play detective and you are setting yourself up for a lousy first impression. The other person's eye will be drawn to the most aesthetically pleasing person. Regardless of your appearance, if you are not that person, all the other people will feel disappointed. Five men were eliminated, leaving the last fifteen that Monica swiped right on. Monica would match with ten of them.

Securing the Date Through Banter and Charm

Congratulations on matching with a real person! Now comes the hard part–keeping them interested. Not only do you have to be an effective communicator, but you also have to be fun and engaging enough for a stranger to come out into the cold and meet with you. It's a tall order when you say it out loud, but you need to remain confident in your skills.

Prime the Pump with a Good Opener

Consider the opening message as your second first impression. The other person's eyes will likely be solely on the chat box from now on, so you need to make it count. An uninspired "hiiiii", a lazy "wyd" or a crass comment will get you unmatched. There is room for flirtiness, but it has to be calibrated to match, if the other person is not interested in a casual relationship, words like "hot", "sexy", or starting with sexual comments lets a person know you are only interested in one thing. Use words like "handsome" or "pretty" to get the ball rolling, and then gauge their temperature as you go. For Monica, *I'll bet you look sexy under that lab coat* does not work nearly as well as *I've always had a thing for women in lab coats.*

You can always up the ante, but once you put them off with a crude joke, there is no unringing that bell.

If you want to stand out, you need to be creative (this is where being more judicious with your right swipes comes into play).

Dig deeper than a lame pun and ask a person about their profiles.

- That dog is so cute! What's his name? Tell me all about him.

- I love the Grateful Dead. What's your go-to song to sing to the belt during a car ride?

- You went to Japan! I have wanted to go. Do you have any travel tips?

- Use one of the clever ice breakers outlined in chapter 2.

- Do you need a belay partner for your next rock climbing workout? How long have you been climbing?

They are open ended questions that show that you read the profile. Even people who are into casual relationships like to be humanized in the apps. A colossal mistake perpetrated by those seeking a purely physical relationship is thinking with their crotch instead of their brain. Even though a relationship is not the goal, sex is still a vulnerable, risky affair.

While you can crank up the dial on flirting, talking like you are the lead in a bad porn movie is not the way to go. Acting pushy, emphasizing how much of a "dom" you are, or inviting a person over immediately will give most self-respecting people the ick.

Of the ten swipes that turned into matches, two sent bad openings, three never responded past the first message, one was only looking for something physical, and two revealed they were incompatible with Monica. One is going on a date with her.

So, What Makes a Good Profile?

A good profile for both men and women is—first and foremost—honest. The pictures are recent, sans filters, all the information is up to date, and potential deal breakers such as non monogamy or having children are present. Your first picture is of you looking straight at the camera, smiling with teeth; it is scientifically proven to look more attractive.

Don't be afraid to take a selfie here as long as it is not a bathroom mirror selfie. Use the back-facing camera for a more flattering photo. Your prompts will tell a person about your interests and what you are looking for and show them your personality. This should give potential mates enough information that they are starting to get to know you, which inspires trust and gets them to be able to picture themselves with you.

Your pictures are the most critical part. You should be in all of them. Leave out photos of possessions, hobbies, and animals if you are not also in them. Variety is important; profiles are valuable real estate, and every part needs to send a message.

Name: Arthur

Age: 32

Education: Graduate Degree

Occupation: Data Analyst

Height: 5'9"

Location: New York City

Bio: Just a guy looking for someone to explore with. When I am not crunching numbers for the 1% you can find me on my favorite running path, reading, painting, or relaxing with a video game! Hoping to find someone to go snowboarding and cuddle with by the fire.

Why would I make a great plus one: I will win over your grandparents through my natural charisma and my knowledge of senior citizen discounts.

A Pro and Con of Dating me: Con is I can't cook to save my life, pro is that I will happily do the grocery shopping and dishes

My favorite qualities in a person are: Ambition, self-improvement, open-minded, kind heart but is not afraid to call out bullshit.

Photo 1: Arthur is smiling and looking at the camera, posing with a statue at a museum.

Photo 2: Arthur dressed up and surrounded by other professionals at a conference.

Photo 3: Arthur running a marathon.

Photo 4: Arthur playing with his dog.

Photo 5: A more artistic picture of Arthur looking at a bonfire.

What Banter is Not

Banter should never be at one person's expense; it is plain old *negging*. A neg is insulting another person to break them down so you can pick them back up. It can be intentional and taught by pickup artists who have not spoken to another woman in years, or it can be unintentional. You should never tease someone about something they cannot control unless you know they are okay with it. You can see the contradiction; the banter is based on teasing, which inherently involves pointing out flaws. If someone is unprepared for this, it can backfire.

Monica: Hi, my name is Monica; what brings you to my regular watering hole tonight?

Man: My name is Dong; I am just relaxing after a long day of work.

Monica: Dong?! That's a weird name; I'll bet you get a lot of stares when you introduce yourself!

Dong: No, I don't; why would you think that?

Monica: Well, because...this is awkward.

Dong never pointed at his name being a previous object of ridicule; poking fun at him should have been seen as a risk, but Monica dove in any way and paid for it. If Dong had said:

Dong: My name is Dong; you can laugh. It's okay.

Monica could have introduced a bit of light teasing at his and her own expense. If you are having a great time

117

engaging in what you think is banter, but the person starts to shrink or get defensive, you may have gone too far. Banter takes two people, and you risk alienating the person if you overreach to prove how funny you are. It could have a profoundly negative effect even if you did not mean it.

Teasing a person about stereotypes may keep them from sharing their culture or family with you, teasing an earnest attempt to speak a foreign language may destroy their confidence, and joking about another person being unlovable might lead them to believe it as fact. Banter is supposed to be lighthearted; keep it that way.

The Art of Banter

Humor next to united values is one of the best ways to gauge our compatibility with a person. Now, this does not mean we need to know every inside joke to a niche interest like the other person. But being on the same wavelength in tone and levity is huge.

If you are partial to dark humor, engaging with someone like Ned Flanders may not be the move. Banter allows us to be a bit vulnerable without the conversation getting too heavy. However, it is risky if you don't know the person. You don't know their humor threshold or sensitivities. For example, some people who are affected by it are comfortable joking about suicide, others will be uncomfortable.

Becoming effective at banter requires:

- The ability to read body language.
- Active listening.
- Quick thinking.
- Having a wide range of knowledge.
- Good judgment.
- Having a sense of humor about yourself.

No wonder banter is so valued; these qualities have "marriage material" written all over them. Body language and active listening will tell if the person is enjoying the exchange and adjust if they are upping the ante. Banter in real-time can be quick; if you want the momentum to continue, you need to think on your feet and pull from your reservoir of trivia and pop culture references to keep things fresh and to pivot as the topic changes.

Since you are currently reading a book, you probably have this part down. Abraham Lincoln, one of America's greatest and ironically shy presidents, had this down to a science. Despite being a lawyer, then a politician, he was incredibly soft-spoken. Still, he honed his communication style not by talking people's ears off but by reading a lot. He was famously witty, fast on his feet, and effective without being "alpha".

Bantering requires good judgment. To avoid shoving your foot firmly in your mouth, you should start with self-effacing humor. This style of humor is often well-received, and you don't risk insulting the other person.

Arthur: I frequent this bar because I can dull my sense of existential dread on the cheap.

Woman: Oh, I come to this bar to enjoy the atmosphere of people having a crisis.

Arthur: Entertainment on a budget, I see.

Woman: Of course. How else am I going to be amused in this city with all that money I don't have.

Arthur: Don't worry, you are in good company; let me give you more bang for your buck, and let me buy you a beer.

Woman: I'd like that very much; in return, I can offer unsolicited advice that I have no business giving on your crisis.

Arthur: I would appreciate that.

The conversation started with Arthur joking about his presence at the bar and being cheap. The woman, in turn, took that and turned it into a joke about seeking entertainment from dark places because she, too, is cheap. With the financial implication, Arthur can buy her a drink not because he assumed she did not have money (a potentially ego-damaging claim) but because she offered that information. They are now tied together for the rest of the night.

Texting With the Intention of Dating

Your match has not ghosted after the opener; you might have a shot of going on a date. There is a lot of conflicting advice on this part since human behavior varies so much. Some don't mind meeting right away. Others may want to get to know you through text for a little while. Others might be busy with life and cannot drop everything immediately to go out with you. Patience can be a virtue in these cases. More often than not, people that are guarded like this were made that way through unfortunate circumstances. You can often judge people's intentions through text. If they say they would instead communicate on the app but drop to one-word sentences or take a day to respond, they are most likely not interested.

Monica: Hey, do anything fun this weekend?

Man: Not really.

Monica: Do you at least have an exciting week at work coming up?

Man: I guess.

There might be mutual interest if they text you back quickly and initiate conversations. There is no magic number of days to ask to go on a date. However, you don't want to wait too long, either. If the conversation is not accelerating beyond memes and "how are you", it will halt completely unless one of you acts. You should try initiating within a few days of consistent texting. If not, a newer match may come in and monopolize the other person's attention, and you get phased out. Dates should also not be planned too far in advance. You need to seize on your novelty and excitement. Try to schedule something for no later than that weekend. Regardless of the time frame, you must keep talking until the date.

Navigating the First Date

First dates are scary. You are coming face to face with a person who has only been a profile picture and text the whole time. What if they are a catfish, what if they ghost, what if they are an axe murderer – you will find out tonight. Meeting in a public space is key. If you are the type to take the initiative, pick a couple of spots and let the other person make the final pick. Allowing the other person to choose also shows you their values. A cheap dive bar can signify frugality, simple tastes, or trying to get in your pants with as little effort as possible. Choosing a high-end place can indicate the person might have expensive tastes or want a free quality meal. It is on you to discern which is which on a date. Just try to make traveling equitable unless agreed otherwise. Traveling a bit has its advantages. If you are not paying for the date, it can be a way to even out the burden. It also gives you an out if the date is going poorly:

Oh no it's late, I have a long commute and an early morning. Sorry I have to cut this short.

It also gives the other person no information on where you live. With all the boring safety stuff out of the way, how do we handle the first date, assuming the result is not you waking up in a bathtub full of ice with an organ missing?

You sit at a middle-of-the-road cocktail bar with food, a solid choice for a first bar. It implies a bit of class, effort, and the food implies that they are okay spending more time there. Surprise, your date shows up, and they look better than their profile. You quickly give a friendly chaste hug, and now the games begin. You might think this is where you will pull out the banter and keep them on their feet the whole time. Banter, while fun, can be exhausting. Try to settle into a deeper conversation.

Arthur: You came from a modeling gig? I thought you were a web developer.

Woman: It's art modeling. I'm not going to fashion week or anything. It's a side hustle, I don't mind being naked, and the cash is nice. Plus, I might end up in a museum someday.

If Arthur didn't practice active listening, he would have heard the word "naked", and his mind would have gone for the low-hanging fruit in an attempt at banter.

I'll bet you turn on all the students when you pose.

It looks like you aren't as innocent as you look.

Women have it easy; they can take off their clothes and profit!

So that means you wouldn't mind getting naked for me tonight?

With active listening, Arthur picks up on the subtext.

- Modeling is not his date's whole identity; it's more of a hobby.
- She is humble but takes pride in her work.
- Just because the job requires nudity does not mean it is sexual in nature.
- She is not cracking jokes when talking about this.

Forcing sexuality or humor in a statement is a textbook failure of active listening. Arthur wants her to let her guard down, but not at her expense.

Arthur: Still, if I showed up to model for a class, everyone would probably want their money back.

Woman: Haha, I highly doubt that! You'd be surprised at the types of successful people in that line of work.

Arthur: How did you even get into that line of work? Did you think you would be successful?

Instead of the low-hanging fruit, Arthur asked an insightful question and showed that he took his date seriously. He can also gauge how he is doing in the trust department. Depending on the answer, she might still have her walls up, or she is warming up to him. A short answer might spell that Arthur has more work to do.

Eh, I needed the money.

Just seemed like fun.

The more information she offers freely, the better.

Woman: Truth is, I don't think I could have done this a couple of years ago. I was pretty insecure.

Arthur: No way!

Woman: Oh yeah, I was a regular pearl-clutching square.

This is not the time to argue, even if it's in the person's favor; let the conversation flow:

Arthur: So, what changed?

Woman: I realized that my insecurities were holding me back, and incidentally, a trip to your home country of Norway changed my life.

Do not hijack the conversation with your opinions on how you don't believe she could change based on a vacation or going on about your knowledge of a country.

Arthur: Wait, I know Norway is fantastic, but how did that lead to modeling?

Woman: Well, Norway has co-ed saunas. I wanted to pamper myself after a pretty active vacation. Instead of doing the easy thing and picking a woman's only baths,

I wanted to try the co-ed ones. I realized that no one cared about what I looked like; just like that, those thoughts that plagued my mind were gone, and I was comfortable in my skin. When I saw an art school needing a model, I decided why not.

Arthur: That's amazing; I am afraid of mice and what you did was the equivalent of jumping into a sewer full of flesh-eating rats!

Woman: Thank you! You know you are the first person that did not make a sex joke when I told them I modeled.

Arthur: What, me? Never!

Arthur said so little and yet did so much. He guided the conversation to a place where she could open up about her past insecurities. Had he made an ill-placed joke or changed the subject, he never would have gotten her to a place like that.

He also lightened the mood with self-defacing humor and a humorous visual once his date was finished with her piece. Remember, you become attractive to another person when you show that you care about what they say. You have set the tone for the conversation; it may be your turn to show some things about yourself.

Don't be afraid of silence; just enjoy each other's presence and let yourself recharge from the conversation.

Sealing the Deal with Physical Contact

You just got out of your first successful date. You want to end the night on a high note with a kiss, but how do you approach this? If you play it safe, you risk alienating the other person, but if you overshoot, that would just be embarrassing, and you can end up with an acrylic nail embedded in your face.

If you are dating in a new culture, what is considered appropriate public displays of affection can cause culture shock. Western cultures are much more relaxed, as couples often touch, lean on each other, and kiss in public. Relationships also move a lot faster, depending on where you are.

In the west and in especially large American cities. Kissing is normalized around the third date, but some hook up on the first. This contrasts Japanese and Korean culture, which has a much more reserved take on affection. If you go to a new place, it will behoove you to consume media from that part of the world. You can pick up on a lot of cultural nuances and be entertained at the same time.

Men are flat-out not used to physical contact like women are (do not assume women are okay with physical touch). Men receive fewer hugs and are much less likely to engage in physical contact beyond a backslap or a firm handshake, which does not translate well in dating. Women tend to have more intense relationships with their female friends, including lots of hugging, kissing on the cheek, and touching. The point is that physical contact can be intimidating on another level to men because they rarely have a real-world example of how to initiate a hug that is platonic and therefore not a big deal. Combatting this will take some self-awareness, body language reading, and courage.

- Let the woman take the lead. Have they made physical contact with you? Have they jokingly poked you, touched you on the shoulder, and made no effort to create space between the both of you? These are all good signs that she, at the very least, feels comfortable with you.

- Recognize platonic vs. non-platonic touching. If you want to start testing the waters, do not start by touching the face or the lower back. Stick to the arms and the shoulders. These are considered intimate and can send way too strong a signal that can make a woman uncomfortable, especially if it turns out you were wrong about her comfort level.

- Keep it soft and brief, do not attempt to grip too tight or give an unwelcome massage.

- Look into her eyes; if she wants to take it up a notch, she will probably not flinch at some prolonged eye contact.

When you are ready to initiate, you can approach this in several ways. Once in a quieter environment, you can lean in for a hug or kiss. As you do this slowly, the woman should start to close the distance simultaneously. If not, she may recoil and step away. You can also just ask. It may seem weird, but a lot of women appreciate the ability to give verbal consent. Some phrases include:

Do you mind if I hug you?

I would like to kiss you right now. Is that okay?

You are allowing someone agency on whether they get to be touched, something that many have been robbed of at one time or another. If they don't want to, that is perfectly okay. You may have read positive signals perfectly, and they might still say no. Don't take it personally, especially if you have just met this person. Pick yourself up, learn from the experience and try again.

Key Takeaways

- Dating apps are designed to be difficult but they are the easiest way to meet people.

- A great profile will not matter if the first photo is bad.

- Bios need to be creative and show a person who you are, don't skip this step.

- Pictures should show an idealized you engaged in different things.

- Banter is a great tool in dating, but it needs to give way for actual deep conversation.

- Letting a conversation flow naturally rather than waiting for beats to prove how funny you are will give way to trust, tender moments and really learning about the other person.

- Physical contact is hard to master. If you have any doubts let the other person take the lead. Don't be afraid to just ask if the moment is right.

THE ART OF DIFFUSION

"There are plenty of people in funeral homes that had the right of way."

- UNKNOWN

When you talk to enough people, it will go poorly at some point. The other person might be having a terrible day or is simply a jerk. These situations can quickly escalate from a disagreement to a screaming match or even a physical fight. Regardless of the cause, getting out of these situations safely is essential.

In these situations, it's not about being right; it's about ceasing the exchange as soon as possible. This might involve some placating, but it's better than going viral in the next *Karen's Gone Wild* compilation.

Despite changes in approach, there is one constant; you must remain calm. Do not give them any room to up the ante. No matter how intimidating the other person is, never flinch. Stand up tall and keep your hands visible but not balled into a fist. Remember, breaking eye contact signifies submission in our animal brains. Active listening and keeping your cool will keep you safe and sane.

Collecting Role Models: Joe Biden and the 2020 Debates

Regardless of your opinion on politics, an excellent example of meeting hostility head-on and coming out on top was fully displayed during the 2020 presidential debates. Joe Biden was up against an opponent who won the last election by winning over the country in his ability to overpower his opponent on the debate stage. Trump would try it again, insulting Biden, disregarding his son that died of brain cancer and poking fun at his other son with past substance abuse issues. Biden could have gotten defensive:

How dare you talk about my son!

You are lying!

Let's talk about your failings as a husband and father!

All of these were tantalizing choices that would have felt good at the moment but would ultimately give Trump the control he wanted. Instead, Biden fired back not with hostility but with love:

My son, like a lot of people, had a drug problem. He's overtaken it. He's fixed it. He's worked on it. And I'm proud of him. I'm proud of my son.

The exchange backfired on Trump because instead of fighting, Biden rose above. Trump had nowhere to go at that point. The next day that moment was on repeat showing everyone how compassionate Biden was and how petty his opponent was.

Unfortunately, it is easier to escalate than to de-escalate. Escalation is often born of anger, a straightforward, satisfying emotion. Anger tends to overtake more complex thought patterns, such as self-reflection and guilt. You are free to scream and rage to feel like you have some control and are being heard.

Escalation lights up parts of the brain associated with self-image, putting work into the parts associated with pride with the added consequence of riskier behavior. De-escalation decisions are associated with introspective parts of the brain that are more inhibitory, making you less likely to act impulsively. When you are in the heat of the moment, thanks to the wiring in your brain, you will be more likely to escalate due to the more straightforward pathways. You must be conscious of this fact before you do something stupid. Take a breath and attempt to de-escalate.

Sympathetic Route

This is your first line of defense, assuming the other person is having a bad day. You have to make the person realize their anger is a secondary emotion. This person might feel frustrated, cheated, or short on time. It's not an excuse, but it can snap a person out of anger. Let them get it all out; just venting lets people calm down and hear their thought process out loud can help them put things in perspective. They might realize how stupid they look yelling at a teenage employee. Once they finish waiting for a pause and state:

I am so sorry that you were sold a defective phone. This sounds incredibly frustrating, and I want to make it right. I will see what I can do to recover the data so you can, at the very least, get your photos and videos back and repair your phone or see about getting a new one.

The tech got the full scope of the problem by letting the customer talk; it wasn't about the phone; it was about the data on the phone that got them so upset. They validated those emotions and let them know how they would make it right. While it may be true, never tell a customer they are wrong or at fault in the heat of the moment. They now see you as someone on their side who will work to fix the problem instead of a company stooge.

Another tactic is giving people choices (or at least the illusion of choice). These choices can guide a person into doing what you want or, at the very least, calming down since they will see you as an ally. An angry or distressed person will get worse if you rob them of a choice. These types are often placated by having some power.

Do you want to talk here or go outside where it's quieter?

Would you like a drink of water?

Would you like me to help you, or would you like to wait for the manager?

Allowing even the tiniest bit of agency can flip a person since they feel their opinion matters. At this point, the person has calmed down a bit. Now is not your time to seize the moment and say something snarky. Pick your battles and let them go. A person might be walking away feeling shame for their behavior, but if you challenge them, they are vindicated and will learn nothing. It's not about what makes you feel good; it's about the best possible outcome for everyone to go home happy.

Tough Route

The tough route is reserved for those who will not listen to reason. They may be inebriated, amid an extreme emotional reaction, or just a jerk—either way, these types need to be dealt with safely. Odds are the result will favor you more than the other person, so convincing them will be an uphill battle.

People in this state are often not reasoning and will not cooperate with anything you have to say unless you prime them for it. Ask them for their name and use them. Introduce yourself (use a fake name if the situation calls for it). People respond better to hearing their name, and you have extended an olive branch by offering your name. It is harder to dehumanize a person in this state. Repeat the behaviors you want to see from them.

I need you to lower your voice; let's both take it down a notch; I can only help you if you calm down and give me the whole story.

Tell me what's going on, talk to me, explain the situation, and help me understand.

Let me help you; we can fix this; tell me what you want me to do.

It can all be used to attempt to get the person into a state where they are more likely to take direction. You can also use the *foot-in-the-door* technique to get a person accustomed to listening to you by starting small and working your way up. If a person is belligerent, but you need them to listen to you, ask them to do something simple such as sitting down or asking for their name.

Never underestimate the power of getting the person to say 'yes' even if it's just a response to a question. This opens the doors for them to see you as someone they can agree with. These techniques are useful when underneath it, all are still decent people despite their behavior. What if this person will never see reason and runs the risk of harming you, either professionally or physically?

Do not argue or play along. Set a precedent for how this conversation will go. Call out bad behavior while remaining civil if the person is yelling or engaging in unproductive behaviors.

Listen, Deborah, I know you are upset, but yelling and cursing out my staff is not something I can accept. I am trying to help you, but you need to calm down. You can deal with me and fix this now or try and find someone else to help you.

While you are framing it as a choice, it's more of an ultimatum. You are establishing yourself as their only way to get something out of the situation. Even the most combative people have some sense of self-preservation. This can also involve calmly telling someone that you are getting law enforcement involved, or being left in the dust. This is the point of no return. Either the problem gets solved now or never. At this point, if they are still not budging they have no respect for you, which is the one thing you cannot work with.

Key Takeaways

- Approach confrontations assuming the person is having a bad day rather than being malicious...until they prove otherwise.

- Seeking to understand is the best way to make an unreasonable person, easier to deal with.

- Once all hope is lost for an amicable exchange, switch tactics. Talk in a clear commanding tone and do not allow the other person to disrespect you.

- Do not be afraid to cut your losses and abandon the exchange.

BUT WHAT IF I'M SHY?

"Communicating effectively helps in developing relationships with others. It helps in expressing ideas and encourages decision-making in an individual. If one does not train themselves to communicate as effectively as possible, they will experience a lack of confidence and fluent working."

- ADAM GARCIA

Introverts live in an extroverted world as extroverts tend to climb the top of the social ladder and run for office. Introverts are left to flounder as their unease around people can cost them opportunities at work and in dating. You can do some things to get your voice out there and use your quiet nature to your advantage.

Practicing on the Extroverts Playground

When you don't have a lively social life, practicing what it means to be a "people person" is tough. You can model people you admire, but you have to get out there and practice. Ask the cashier at the store a question or compliment the color of their shirt (don't overstay your welcome). Go to a place with live music so you will have something in common with everyone there and strike up a conversation. You will likely never see those people again, so you can take a couple of risks.

If you want to practice talking to the opposite gender in a dating setting, there is a solution that is often slept on– speed dating. Go to an event (they are even hosted online now) with no expectations. There you can practice talking to several people very quickly. You can work on your conversation skills and read the person's body language to see how they react. The more you do it, the less scary it becomes.

Join a creative or fitness class. Surround yourself with like-minded people with similar aspirations. You don't have to be best friends but try making an effort to talk about your work and ask people about theirs. You don't have to worry about conversation openers and figuring out what makes this person tick because you have your answer.

Getting Comfortable with Eye Contact

Eye contact that is confident but not overbearing is a difficult thing, especially if you are anxious, to begin with. Practice makes perfect. Make brief eye contact with people on the street, enough that the eyes meet but not so much that you have to turn your head. Do not acknowledge the other person; this is about getting acclimated to eye contact.

Practice maintaining eye contact with anyone you have a casual interaction with. When ordering in a restaurant, stop looking at your menu while speaking to the waitress. Remember to relax. You don't want to freak out a poor service worker by looking like you are undressing them with your stare. Think of it as budget exposure therapy.

Practicing at Work

Being quiet is not the best quality for a worker looking to move up. While it is tempting to disappear into the bushes and let someone else do the talking, you will never grow socially or professionally. Take ownership of your work whenever you can. If someone is confused, be the one to explain it. You will get a voice and insight to see if your communication style effectively delivers information.

Being able to synthesize your point properly is not easy when you are shy, but it's even worse with the weight of high expectations and a hundred pairs of eyeballs staring at you. You can start small by asking questions at the end of a presentation. Ideally, it would be something that pertains to your area of work, but you can also ask about the pitfalls of the process and what the most important lesson they learned was. This question has three parts, complimenting the project, identifying a potential problem point, and asking the speaker for advice.

This project had a lot of moving parts. Can I ask if you ran into any trouble trying to juggle it all and how you adjusted your pipeline?

If your goal is to be in charge, you have to get used to the idea that you will have to present at some point. How many managers do you see toiling away with the other worker bees? Not many. That is because they are busy being the friendly face of their department. You have to do some Neuro Linguistic Programming on yourself. Reframe your thoughts and think about how you will succeed. You have to stop telling yourself and others:

I'm stupid!

Why am I giving this talk? I am the wrong person for this.

Everyone will see how dumb I am.

I can't do this.

Don your "I know more than you" persona and get to work. You will set up your visual aids to be clear and concise. This is not just for the audience but for you as well. You will not fall into the trap of having every bit of information on a slide that is now too overwhelming to read. You won't need it because you will practice this presentation alone and in front of a trusted colleague. Once they help you, it is unlikely you will be caught by surprise by a typo or a wrong bit of information, so you can let that stress go.

Finally, use that empathy that you have learned. Based on the presentation I just gave, ask yourself what question would Craig, who asks questions at every talk have? Are there any weaknesses in my methods, or information gaps? How should I answer them? Finally, you have the escape hatch.

That's an excellent question that we are still looking into. We will let you know when we have an answer.

Or even better:

That's a great question that I don't have an answer to; I will get back to you on that!

Even esteemed professors with degrees from Harvard have used that gem; it is also okay for you to use it.

Embracing Your Quiet Nature

Not everyone in this world is an extrovert, and that's okay because this world would be obnoxious if that were the case. It takes a certain confidence to feel like you don't need to fill in every silence. Introverts can be less predictable and are often underestimated since they don't display their motivations or need for external validation quite so openly. You can use all of this to your advantage.

It's always the quiet ones that are often said in jest, but extroverts can live in fear of the right introvert. Since introverts tend to keep things to themselves, when you do say something, it carries a lot of weight. That is power and can steer a conversation if you use it sparingly. Your voice is to be respected. All you need to do is open with firmness and a bit more volume and return to your usual demeanor at the next line. No one likes it when the quiet guy is angry, especially if they respect the quiet guy. If your reactionary, cranky boss is angry at you, even if they are in the right, you won't be bothered because they are always upset. When you disappoint or upset a quiet person, especially if you usually like this person, you tend to be ashamed and want to fix the mistake as soon as possible.

Never set a precedent for people to step on you in meetings or conversations. People that feel the need to do so maliciously tend to seek out people that they think will not push back. If you give them any resistance, these types will probably back off, especially if you have the respect of your team. Remember the tips on handling meeting interruptions and de-escalation. Use a clear voice and a small gesture to let them know this is still your time. Never let this behavior go unchecked.

You live in silence, you thrive in it, and you can use it. People find silence uncomfortable and will fill it with nonsense rather than exist in it. Once you deliver a point, let people stew in it. Silence makes people squirm; they will offer information you never asked for or balk.

Key Takeaways

- Having a quiet nature is a strength if you know how to use it.

- Being comfortable in silence is a great tool when communicating in high stress situations.

- You need to inoculate yourself into getting used to talking and eye contact. Speed dating and making an effort to look at someone when they talk will go a long way.

- We are taught that being outwardly brash is a strength, and quietness is weakness, you have to deprogram yourself from those thoughts.

CONCLUSION

There are a lot of tips and tricks to becoming more social both in real life and behind a screen. Most of them boil down to demonstrating a confident open nature. You do not need to do a complete personality overhaul, you just need to recognize that extroverted nature as a mode in your personality you can call on. Moving up in the world requires the ability to talk to anyone. Finding charm, wit, and confidence within yourself will make communication easier.

Talking is probably the least important part of all of this. Prioritize learning how to listen. Find the meaning between the lines demonstrated by how a person talks, their disposition, what they say and what they don't. Let go of that need to contribute, reinforce and ask follow up questions. Once you learn to do that, you can actually start mastering your own style of communication, now that you have the tools to know what to say and how.

Start with your body language. Walk around spaces like you would in your own home, because you belong there. Take up space, speak with self assurance and feel safe enough to take some risks. Mirror this attitude and project it back to others so they will feel the same way about you and maybe even themselves.

Don't be afraid to start talking and get into those deep conversations. You become interesting by showing interest in the other person. Some active listening and the ability to ask good thought provoking questions will create that elusive rapport that can end in friendship.

Be that confident person everywhere, at work and at play but recognize how to adjust to your environment. Our ability to communicate not only affects us, but everyone around us. Confidence is not easy and it takes energy, take a rest if you need it.

As you model yourself after people whose communication style resonated with you, in time it gets easier. Those traits will become yours as people react positively to them. The more positive social interactions you have, the more diluted any bad ones become. Don't give up and keep practicing. Practice in person and online so you know exactly how you come across regardless of the format. Once you get comfortable, start peppering in banter and have fun.

Humans are social creatures and we are supposed to thrive with human connection. Just because you might be a bit shy, does not mean you need to be deprived of those joys. There is no timeline for success, start small and never stop surprising yourself with what you can do.

Thank You for Reading

Did you know that you are in the top percentage of readers in the world? You committed to reading a book and have made it through to the end. Congratulations for having and exercising a *success mindset*!

While you're here and seeing as communication is the subject of this book, it would be absolutely fantastic if you could spare a moment of your time to communicate with me by leaving a short review.

If you do have the time to leave one for me, I will be eternally grateful! Scan a QR Code below and go directly to your Amazon review page. Log into your account *(if you aren't already)* and in under a minute it'll be done.

Amazon Review US

Amazon Review UK

If you don't have time now, that's no problem at all. You can always come back to it later if you would like to.

Have an awesome day!

- *Lucas*

Remember to download your 2 free eBooks from
https://bit.ly/lucasbaileybonus

REFERENCES

A Shy Person's Guide to Making Yourself Heard In a Group Conversation. (2015, January13).Lifehacker. https://lifehacker.com/a-shy-persons-guide-to-making-yourself-heard-in-a-group-1679102536

Adelman, L., & Verkuyten, M. (2019). Rules of engagement: Reactions to internal and external criticism in public debate. *British Journal of Social Psychology.* https://doi.org/10.1111/bjso.12351

American Psychological Association. (2017). Prolonged Exposure (PE). Https://Www.apa.org. https://www.apa.org/ptsd-guideline/treatments/prolonged-exposure

Analysis: Trump leans on tone that turns off voters he needs. (2020, September 30). AP NEWS. https://apnews.com/article/election-2020-joe-biden-virus-outbreak-donald-trump-chris-wallace-20c2c6d892bbae83aa49a49e8a431011

Aspy, D. N., Roebuck, F. N., & *National Consortium For Humanizing Education.* (1983). Kids don't learn from people they don't like. Human Resource Development Press.

Ball Cooper, E., Anderson, J. L., Sharp, C., Langley, H. A., & Venta, A. (2021). Attachment, Mentalization, and Criterion B of the Alternative DSM-5 Model for Personality Disorders (AMPD). *Borderline Personality Disorder and Emotion Dysregulation,* 8(1). https://doi.org/10.1186/s40479-021-00163-9

Banter with care. (n.d.). Conversational Leadership. Retrieved December 20, 2022, from https://conversational-leadership.net/banter/

Begemann, V., Lübstorf, S., Meinecke, A. L., Steinicke, F., & Lehmann-Willenbrock, N. (2021). Capturing Workplace Gossip as Dynamic Conversational Events: First Insights From Care Team Meetings. *Frontiers in Psychology,* 12. https://doi.org/10.3389/fpsyg.2021.725720

Bergman, C., Dellve, L., & Skagert, K. (2016). Exploring communication processes in workplace meetings: A mixed methods study in a Swedish healthcare organization. Work, 54(3), 533–541. ncbi. https://doi.org/10.3233/wor-162366

Bligh, M. C., & Kohles, J. C. (2009). The enduring allure of charisma: How Barack Obama won the historic 2008 presidential election. *The Leadership Quarterly*, 20(3), 483–492. https://doi.org/10.1016/j.leaqua.2009.03.013

Body Language to De-escalate. (n.d.). WARN International. https://www.warninternational.com/blog/2015/3/26/body-language-to-de-escalate

Borek, A. J., & Abraham, C. (2018). How do Small Groups Promote Behaviour Change? An Integrative Conceptual Review of Explanatory Mechanisms. *Applied Psychology: Health and Well-Being*, 10(1), 30–61. https://doi.org/10.1111/aphw.12120

Brooks, A. B. J., Herrmann, P. L., & Andreas, S. (2020). The use of banter in psychotherapy: A systematic literature review. *Counselling and Psychotherapy Research*. https://doi.org/10.1002/capr.12361

Bruno, D., Mueller, K. D., Betthauser, T., Chin, N., Engelman, C. D., Christian, B., Koscik, R. L., & Johnson, S. C. (2020). Serial position effects in the Logical Memory Test: Loss of primacy predicts amyloid positivity. *Journal of Neuropsychology*, 15(3), 448–461. https://doi.org/10.1111/jnp.12235

Buglass, S. L., Abell, L., Betts, L. R., Hill, R., & Saunders, J. (2020). Banter Versus Bullying: a University Student Perspective. *International Journal of Bullying Prevention.* https://doi.org/10.1007/s42380-020-00085-0

Conway, C. A., Jones, B. C., DeBruine, L. M., & Little, A. C. (2007). Evidence for adaptive design in human gaze preference. *Proceedings of the Royal Society B: Biological Sciences,* 275(1630), 63–69. https://doi.org/10.1098/rspb.2007.1073

Duford, T.-B. (2018, January 26). Female vs Male Friendships. Psych Central. https://psychcentral.com/blog/relationship-corner/2018/01/female-vs-male-friendships-10-key-differences

Dynamics Of Regular Group Conversations | www.succeedsocially.com. (2022). Succeedsocially.com. https://www.succeedsocially.com/regulargroup conversations

Exploring the Differences Between Male and Female Friendships | Psychology Today. (n.d.).www.psychologytoday.com. https://www.psychologytoday.com/us/blog/ha ppiness-is-state-mind/202112/exploring-the-differences-between-male-and-female-friendships

REFERENCES

Exposure and Desensitization. (n.d.). https://medicine.umich.edu/sites/default/files/ content/downloads/Exposure-and-Desensitization.pdf

Goulston, M. (2015). *Just listen : discover the secret to getting through to absolutely anyone.* Amacom.

Green, K., Kukan, Z., & Tully, R. J. (2017). Public perceptions of "negging": lowering women's self-esteem to increase the male's attractiveness and achieve sexual conquest. *Journal of Aggression, Conflict and Peace Research*, 9(2), 95–105. https://doi.org/10.1108/jacpr-06-2016-0235

Greitemeyer, T. (2007). What do men and women want in a partner? Are educated partners always more desirable? *Journal of Experimental Social Psychology*, 43(2), 180–194. https://doi.org/10.1016/j.jesp.2006.02.006

Groen, D., & Canada, R. D. (n.d.). *The Surprising Science Behind Friendship.* Reader's DigestCanada. https://www.readersdigest.ca/health/relationsh ips/surprising-science-behind-friendship/

Hailey, L. (2022a, May 2). *Be an Expert at Witty Banter...How to Charm With Your Words.* Science of People. https://www.scienceofpeople.com/witty-banter/

Hailey, L. (2022b, August 4). 160 *Best Tinder Conversation Starters For Instant Responses.*

Science of People.
https://www.scienceofpeople.com/tinder-conversation-starters/

Hoption, C., Barling, J., & Turner, N. (2013). "It's not you, it's me": transformational leadership and self-deprecating humor. *Leadership & Organization Development Journal*, 34(1), 4–19. https://doi.org/10.1108/01437731311289947

How Tinder "Feedback Loop" Forces Men and Women into Extreme Strategies. (n.d.). MIT Technology Review.
https://www.technologyreview.com/2016/07/15/158803/how-tinder-feedback-loop-forces-men-and-women-into-extreme-strategies/

How to Have Better Group Conversations | Psychology Today. (n.d.). Www.psychologytoday.com. Retrieved December 18, 2022, from https://www.psychologytoday.com/us/blog/adventures-in-divergent-thinking/202107/how-have-better-group-conversations

July 15, R. B. P. |, & article, 2009 P. (2009, July 15). *How can teachers foster self-esteem in children?* Parenting. https://www.greatschools.org/gk/articles/teachers-foster-self-esteem-in-children/

Karaer, Y., & Akdemir, D. (2019). Parenting styles, perceived social support and emotion regulation in adolescents with internet addiction.

Comprehensive Psychiatry, 92. https://doi.org/10.1016/j.comppsych.2019.03.003

Kohpeima Jahromi, V., Tabatabaee, S. S., Esmaeili Abdar, Z., & Rajabi, M. (2016). Active listening: the Key of Successful Communication in Hospital Managers. *Electronic Physician*, 8(3), 2123–2128. NCBI. https://doi.org/10.19082/2123

Krems, J. A., & Wilkes, J. (2019). Why are conversations limited to about four people? A theoretical exploration of the conversation size constraint. *Evolution and Human Behavior*, 40(2), 140–147. https://doi.org/10.1016/j.evolhumbehav.2018.09.004

Li, L. (2021, July 12). *6 Easy and Effective Ways to Build Team Rapport.* TINYpulse. https://www.tinypulse.com/blog/how-to-build-team-rapport

Liang, T.-P., Li, Y.-W., Yen, N.-S., Turel, O., & Hsu, S.-M. (2021). Framing and self-responsibility modulate brain activities in decision escalation. *BMC Neuroscience*, *22(1)*. https://doi.org/10.1186/s12868-021-00625-4

Longman, M. (n.d.). "I'm Proud Of My Son": *Here's Why Biden's Openness About His Son's Addiction Matters.* Www.refinery29.com. Retrieved December 17, 2022, from https://www.refinery29.com/en-us/2020/09/10062158/hunter-biden-drug-problem-addiction-recovery-joe-debate

Lux, K. M., Hutcheson, J. B., & Peden, A. R. (2014). Ending disruptive behavior: Staff nurse recommendations to nurse educators. *Nurse Education in Practice, 14(1)*, 37–42. https://doi.org/10.1016/j.nepr.2013.06.014

Master Group Conversations. (2019, November 20). Get the Friends You Want. https://getthefriendsyouwant.com/group-conversations/

McLeod, S. (2008). *Serial Position Effect | Simply Psychology.* Simplypsychology.org. https://www.simplypsychology.org/primacy-recency.html

Merriam-Webster. (2019). *Definition of CHARISMA.* Merriam-Webster.com. https://www.merriam-webster.com/dictionary/charisma

Milojevich, H. M., Machlin, L., & Sheridan, M. A. (2020). Early adversity and children's emotion regulation: Differential roles of parent emotion regulation and adversity exposure. *Development and Psychopathology, 32(5)*, 1788–1798. https://doi.org/10.1017/s0954579420001273

Moreira, F. T. L. D. S., Callou, R. C. M., Albuquerque, G. A., & Oliveira, R. M. (2019). Effective communication strategies for managing disruptive behaviors and promoting patient safety. *Revista Gaucha de Enfermagem, 40(spe),* e20180308. https://doi.org/10.1590/1983-1447.2019.20180308

Nelson, D. (2017). How Does Tinder Work: The Science And Psychology Behind Tinder. *Science Trends.* https://doi.org/10.31988/scitrends.5912

NERIS Analytics Limited. (2015, August 25). *Introverted Leaders in History.* 16personalities.com; NERIS Analytics Limited. https://www.16personalities.com/articles/introverted-leaders-in-history

1 *Recommendations | Violence and aggression: short-term management in mental health, health and community settings* | Guidance | NICE. (2015, May 28). Nice.org.uk; NICE. https://www.nice.org.uk/guidance/ng10/chapter/recommendations#terms-used-in-this-guideline

Positive Action. (2021, February 26). 9 *Effective Teaching Strategies for Students With Emotional and Behavioral Disorders.* Www.positiveaction.net. https://www.positiveaction.net/blog/teaching-strategies-for-emotional-and-behavioral-disorders

Prem. (2020, August 6). *Discussing Hollywood's accent discrimination problem.* Www.laineygossip.com. https://www.laineygossip.com/discussing-hollywoods-accent-discrimination-problem/66797

Price, O., Baker, J., Bee, P., & Lovell, K. (2018). The support-control continuum: An investigation of staff perspectives on factors influencing the success or failure of de-escalation techniques for the management of violence and aggression in mental health settings. *International Journal of Nursing Studies, 77(1),* 197–206. https://doi.org/10.1016/j.ijnurstu.2017.10.002

Purtill, C. (2018, September 13). Why can't more than four people have a conversation at once? Quartz. https://qz.com/work/1388086/why-cant-more-than-four-people-have-a-conversation-at-once

Rogelberg, S. G., Allen, J. A., Shanock, L., Scott, C., & Shuffler, M. (2010). Employee satisfaction with meetings: A contemporary facet of job satisfaction. *Human Resource Management, 49(2),* 149–172. https://doi.org/10.1002/hrm.20339

Rogelberg, S. G., Leach, D. J., Warr, P. B., & Burnfield, J. L. (2006). "Not Another Meeting!" Are Meeting Time Demands Related to Employee Well-Being?. *Journal of Applied Psychology,* 91(1),

83–96.   https://doi.org/10.1037/0021-9010.91.1.83

Schwarzenegger, A., Petre, P., Van, T., & Al, E. (2012). Total recall. Vip.

6 Ways To Increase Social Connection At Work. (n.d.). Www.linkedin.com. Retrieved December 20, 2022, from https://www.linkedin.com/pulse/6-ways-increase-social-connection-work-samantha-sellwood

Smith, G. (2020, November 25). *25 Secrets to Sending the Perfect First Message on a Dating App.* Men's   Health. https://www.menshealth.com/sex-women/g22090242/how-to-start-first-tinder-message/?slide=22

The Problem With Telling Women to Email Like Men. (n.d.).   Www.vice.com. https://www.vice.com/en/article/8xyb5v/how-to-write-professional-work-email-women

The sexist expectations of professional emails for women: "There's no winning." (n.d.). Global News. https://globalnews.ca/news/5270439/emails-workplace-etiquette-gender-imbalance-emojis-exclamation-points/

13.3 Small Group Dynamics. (2016, September 29). Open.lib.umn.edu; University of *Minnesota Libraries Publishing edition*, 2016. This edition adapted from a work originally produced in 2013 by a publisher who has requested that it not receive attribution. https://open.lib.umn.edu/communication/chapter/13-3-small-group-dynamics/

Vanessa Van Edwards. (2016, March 28). 10 Science-Backed First Date Tips To Make Your Date... Science of People; Science of People. https://www.scienceofpeople.com/first-date-tips/

Véronneau-Veilleux, F., Robaey, P., Ursino, M., & Nekka, F. (2022). A mechanistic model of ADHD as resulting from dopamine phasic/tonic imbalance during reinforcement learning. *Frontiers in Computational Neuroscience*, 16. https://doi.org/10.3389/fncom.2022.849323

Wainwright, D., Harris, M., & Wainwright, E. (2019). How does "banter" influence trainee doctors' choice of career? A qualitative study. BMC Medical Education, 19(1). https://doi.org/10.1186/s12909-019-1531-0

Werner, A. M., Tibubos, A. N., Rohrmann, S., & Reiss, N. (2019). The clinical trait self-criticism and its relation to psychopathology: A systematic review Update. *Journal of Affective Disorders, 246,* 530–547. https://doi.org/10.1016/j.jad.2018.12.069

What Is Banter? Examples And Applications For Your Relationship | ReGain. (n.d.). Www.regain.us. https://www.regain.us/advice/general/what-is-banter-examples-and-applications-for-your-relationship/

Zabel, S., Vinan Navas, G. T., & Otto, S. (2022). Social norms and webcam use in online meetings. *Frontiers in Psychology*, 13. https://doi.org/10.3389/fpsyg.2022.907405

Zelizer, J. E. (n.d.). *The 8 Biggest Unforced Errors in Debate History*. POLITICO Magazine. https://www.politico.com/magazine/story/201 6/09/presidential-debates-errors-mistakes-gaffes-biggest-history-214279/

Printed in the USA
CPSIA information can be obtained
at www.ICGtesting.com
LVHW092139051023
760329LV00031B/664

9 781739 669041